I0896042

Praise for *Muted Cry*

While many memoirs tell a story of travail, Caroline J. Simon does something more complicated in this compelling personal narrative. Weaving together the family dynamics caused by a suffering sibling and the philosophy of Simone Weil, Simon takes us deep inside the problem of our role as witness. Who are we and what difference can we make when someone we love is in affliction and we can't get them out?

—**Amy Frykholm**, journalist, scholar, and author

Redolent of Will Campbell's *Brother to a Dragonfly* and C. S. Lewis's *A Grief Observed*, Caroline J. Simon's *Muted Cry* unites memoir, prose elegy, and Christian meditation in touching witness to her brother Bill's affliction. Her truth-telling—about Bill, herself, their trials, and God's love in Christ—bears the marks of anguish and heroism, and also of hard-won wisdom and abiding faith. *Muted Cry* is a rare gift in its honesty and a moving invitation to see, *really* see, affliction even when it frightens and dismays.

—**Douglas Henry**, dean of the Honors College,
Baylor University

With clear and vivid descriptions, Caroline J. Simon throws open a window into her brother Bill's life of affliction. As Carol cares for Bill, she struggles to navigate chasms of disparity—of education, personality, and finances—raising valuable questions about what love looks like in practice. Simone Weil's evocative perspective on affliction, woven throughout, enhances the narrative's insight.

—**Lynne M. Baab**, pastor, scholar, and author of
Sabbath Keeping: Finding Freedom in the Rhythms of Rest and *Nurturing Hope: Christian Pastoral Care in the Twenty-First Century*

Simone Weil's reflections on affliction are among her most illuminating and important contributions to Christian spirituality. Caroline J. Simon's lucid and beautiful book brings a philosopher's clarity and a devoted sibling's wisdom to this extraordinary material. Simon's explorations elucidate and personalize Weil's thought in remarkable ways, and they offer unusually helpful guidance for anyone who desires to come alongside someone caught in the grip of affliction. This is a wonderful achievement.

—**Adam Neder**, professor of theology and associate dean of the College of Liberal Arts and Social Sciences, Belmont University

Should we, can we, love those in our lives who are dysfunctional, alcoholic, inconsiderate, or unappreciative? Philosopher Caroline J. Simon lived those questions as her brother Bill's only family member—eliciting her support and her unmerited grace. Her well-told story bids us all to consider what Christ's command to love our neighbor, even the least of these, might mean for us.

—**David Myers**, professor of psychology, Hope College, and author of *How Do We Know Ourselves? Curiosities and Marvels of the Human Mind*

I know of very few books that have been able to portray, concretely and in real life, what Simone Weil called "affliction," and to use Weil to shed light on this dark devastation of the soul. Caroline J. Simon is one of those rare writers to have done so, and to have done so well.

—**Eric O. Springsted**, author of *Simone Weil for the Twenty-First Century* and cofounder of the American Weil Society

The memoir is a medium of writing fraught with peril. Rarely is it done well. Caroline J. Simon is one of the few who has succeeded, as *Muted Cry* shows on every page. It drew me in and kept me there. She tells the story of her brother's long decline and death. It is his story, and hers too. Simon also draws on the story of another, the

French philosopher Simone Weil, especially her deep reflections on "affliction," the physical and psychological equivalent of a multisystem organ failure. She tells the truth about his and her experience, as harrowing and intense as it is. He is the victim of affliction, she the suffering and confused witness. *Muted Cry* is an extraordinary piece of writing. I don't know many people who could have written it. Caroline J. Simon is one of them.

—**Gerald L. Sittser**, professor emeritus of theology, Whitworth University; author of *A Grace Disguised* and *Water from a Deep Well*

MUTED CRY

Caroline J. Simon

MUTED CRY

A Witness to Affliction

FORTRESS PRESS
MINNEAPOLIS

MUTED CRY
A Witness to Affliction

30 29 28 27 26 25 1 2 3 4 5 6 7 8 9

Library of Congress Control Number: 2025022918 (print)

Cover image: Polaroid photograph of sycamore seed in black and white - stock photo from robert reader/Getty Images
Cover design: Kris E. Miller

Print ISBN: 979-8-3419-0027-1
eBook ISBN: 979-8-3419-0028-8

For Wes, Vera, Bill, and Diana, in gratitude
for the love we shared as best we knew how

Hope

waits beside a pool

it cannot fathom

sensing the rubble

it crawled from under

can become a foundation

that its groans are the bass clef

of a symphony's first movement

that holiness hides even here

among the haunted

Contents

Author's Note

This book grapples with one of the grittiest problems of ordinary life: how to come alongside those whose afflictions alienate them from others and from themselves. Because affliction is a complex form of suffering that uproots a life by damaging a person physically, psychologically, socially, and spiritually, it overwhelms the afflicted and baffles those around them. It certainly baffled me. Though I had long been familiar with the brilliant early twentieth-century French philosopher Simone Weil's writings on affliction, it was only in hindsight, after his death, that what she had to say cast light on my blue-collar brother Bill's murky miseries.

This book's narrative brings you along on my journey of growing realization of how Bill became who he was—a slow process, given our family culture of not telling. I have gone against the grain of my upbringing by writing this book, hoping to help you be better prepared than I was to recognize affliction when it arises in your own life or the lives of those around you.

Like many stories of affliction, this one is largely undramatic. Its narrative tension hinges upon the question at the heart of all encounters with the afflicted: Will those around them come to understand them soon enough to be of genuine help? I bring Simone Weil's voice into the narrative at junctures where, in hindsight, I wish she had been whispering in my ear. (If you're puzzled about my wanting her voice in my ear, you might want to read "Why Simone Weil?" on page 135 before proceeding.)

Why tell you a story rather than write a how-to book on helping the afflicted or a treatise on affliction? Because treating someone as a "case" of affliction is to spiritually pass them by, even if you are physically loading them onto a donkey to take them to the inn. Weil thought that those who are afflicted need more than our material help. What they most need from us is our attention—not our analysis or diagnosis but our empathetic imagination. Stories hone this capacity.

Some stories do this more effectively than others. Although Russell Banks's gripping novel, *Affliction*, became the basis for a compelling movie, it falls short as an aid for developing empathy. The novel's main character, Wade Whitehouse, suffers a cascade of losses that triggers murderous rage. Banks's readers may be apt to fear the afflicted because there's no telling what might set them off. Banks quotes Simone Weil in an epigraph, but she had no interest in making us suspect that affliction is the explanation behind sensational headlines. While she acknowledges that our natural reaction to affliction is fear, she thought our fear arises from the reminder that "an accident can at any time wipe out what I am and can indifferently put in its place any vile and contemptible thing." Even when our lives are going smoothly, we are always on the verge of affliction.

No one will buy the movie rights to this book. My brother and I are far too ordinary to attract Hollywood's interest. A warning before you begin: Only those heroically devoted to truth refrain from fictionalizing their pasts to align with their need to see themselves in a flattering light. I have no grounds for thinking I'm an exception to this. In the following narrative, I'll do my best not to deceive you—but be forewarned. Watch out for where I am deceiving myself.

Introduction

I got off the return flight six days after my brother Bill's death in September 2020 angrier than I could remember ever having been. The direct focus of my anger was the jerk who'd sat next to me on the plane. Half the time his mask dangled around his neck; the rest of the time it hung well below his nose. But my anger was out of proportion, even in those pre-vaccine days when masking or not masking was a source of rage.

I've read that anger is one of the stages of grief, so it was natural for me to ask myself whether that was what I was feeling, perhaps heightened because the COVID pandemic had sapped my resiliency. Yet as I palpated my anger, I detected lumps of moral indignation. Some part of me was reacting to a deep wrong. My anger felt like the oddity at a crime scene—the one that becomes not just a clue, but the key to unlocking some mystery.

Good mysteries require multiple suspects. Let me give you an initial sketch of the lineup in this case, to be filled in as the story unfolds.

My brother Bill Miller had spent six years as one of over two hundred thousand people in the United States receiving ongoing dialysis, a multibillion-dollar industry. He had also spent multiple years on the kidney donation candidate list, and stretches of time on Medicaid, on what used to be called welfare (now called SSI—Supplemental Security Insurance), on disability, and on Medicare. Was the wrong that I was reacting to embedded in the injustices endemic to these large-scale systems? Perhaps.

Bill was admittedly not the most responsible, self-disciplined, prudent person. Was my moral indignation triggered by what Bill's faults had cost him and the collateral costs they'd inflicted on me? It's possible.

Another hypothesis is that my anger was self-directed. One of Jesus's most well-known stories is usually called the Parable of the Prodigal Son, though it's about two sons. Their father wanted desperately for them both to come home and stay home, to be reconciled with each other. In Jesus's telling, as soon as one son returns, the other leaves. Were my brother and I enacting a version of this story—my brother, the prodigal, and I, his self-righteous sibling? Much as I dislike thinking I'm a stingy, judgmental prig, part of me periodically suspects that's true. At such times, my self-directed ire is aggravated by knowing I am not in the best position to judge. What we think we know about ourselves and others is often composed of self-serving yarns.

I have come to believe that whatever else this story is about, it can help us ponder the mystery of affliction—a morally important and much-neglected concept. Affliction involves not just physical and emotional suffering, but social and spiritual dislocation. Simone Weil calls it "the great enigma of human life," and distinguishes it from pain, suffering, and sorrow. Pain, suffering, and sorrow often incapacitate us but leave us intact after they pass. Affliction leaves a person undone. "Soul destroying" is, for most users, a metaphorical expression. When Weil talks about affliction destroying souls, she invites us to take her seriously.

A new book or article on trauma appears almost weekly: childhood trauma, intergenerational trauma, everyday trauma. Books about affliction are rare, though Weil thought that affliction hides in plain sight all around us. One reason for the hiddenness of affliction is that it renders the afflicted inarticulate. But the more important reason that affliction remains stubbornly enigmatic is our desperate, mostly unconscious, desire not to see. The roots of our desperation lie in our complicity in allowing customs and practices that plunge others into affliction. Our complicity comes in many forms: cowardice, inertia, and culpable ignorance. "It is certain that each of us is involved at least in the guilt of criminal indifference," says Weil.

Conjecturing affliction as a prime suspect in Bill Miller's story need not lead us to eliminate other culprits. Affliction has many minions. This contributes to its ability to hide. Structural injustice, criminal indifference, lovelessness, and even the afflicted themselves number among those minions, at least potentially, according to Weil.

A roster of suspects is not an indictment. As you read, make up your own mind about Simone Weil's ideas, and about my brother, and about me. In the end, even if you doubt that affliction was my brother's assailant, or even his stalker, what you learn about affliction as this tale unfolds will expand your capacity to attend to the afflicted.

Paying real attention to the afflicted is costly. Weil says it always entails self-loss. Why, then, would you want to enhance your awareness of this condition? For Weil, affliction is a key theological term. Understanding affliction opens our eyes to deep truths about Christ, about humanity, and about how to follow Christ in God's precious, broken creation. To the extent that we remain blind or indifferent to affliction, we flatten and falsify the world.

Yet, an interest in theology is not a prerequisite for finding Weil's subtle and psychologically rich descriptions of affliction insightful. Because Weil thought her peculiar calling was to witness from "the intersection of Christianity and everything that is not Christianity," much of what she has to say on most topics is worthy of consideration by thoughtful people of many faiths or none. You may in the end disagree with her, but she will not waste your time.

All human lives are particular—even peculiar—but they are also intertwined, however distantly. I'm neither an ancient Roman North African nor a first-generation Chinese American, yet Augustine's story in his *Confessions* about his boyhood raid on a neighbor's orchard and the story that Maxine Hong Kingston tells of her no-name aunt in *The Warrior Woman* both give me what Kingston calls ancestral help. Perhaps you yourself have been afflicted or tried to help someone who is. Perhaps you, like many contemporary Americans, think that affliction happens seldom and always far away. Whatever your circumstances, I hope that this story of two siblings will spur you to ask how affliction's enigmas pertain to your own life. Those are questions you alone, or in some cases God alone, can answer.

CHAPTER 1

Careening Downhill

My brother and I talked more during the last six years of his life than in the prior four decades combined. That was after Bill almost died—after, in some moods, he would say I almost killed him.

My part in all that started on a June day in 2014 with my cell phone vibrating in a meeting. When I saw that the call was from Bill, I suspected it was what he'd call a butt-dial. My brother was not an initiator—or even much of a responder. Mundane courtesies eluded him. Every year I'd been sending him a birthday card, as siblings do. His birthday was five days before mine. Receiving my card could have nudged him to send me a card. No card ever came.

I was three-quarters through an all-day meeting of provosts from Washington's private universities when I missed Bill's call. Gonzaga University was hosting the event. Lesser-known Whitworth University, where I had been provost and executive vice president for just a year, is out on Spokane's fringe between its northern suburbs and the countryside. I'd given a talk during my campus interview for Whitworth's provostship called "Minding the Gap." I'd said that the job of a chief academic officer was to keep her university honest by working toward conforming its daily realities to its lofty self-descriptions. Though I did not know it yet, I was embarking on a six-year journey through the gaps separating my own ideals from my realities. Professionally, the gaps would feel like gullies. In my personal life, they would feel more like crevasses.

During a break, I called Bill back. When he didn't pick up, I left a message saying I'd try again. I made several attempts that evening to reach him, getting his voicemail each time. After still getting no answer the next morning, I called the police in Bill's Portland suburb and asked them to do a welfare check. I pictured this becoming one of those things I'd never live down. Bill periodically saying *Remember that time you called the police on me?*

My husband Steve and I were walking our dog in meadowlands near the Little Spokane River when my cell phone rang. Not Bill's number. Not Bill calling to say *Geez, Carol, do you think I can't take care of myself*? I watched Steve pacing back and forth with Bella as I listened. The voice said they did not find Mr. Miller at home, but they'd found out that paramedics had responded to a 911 call he'd made the prior afternoon before he'd lost consciousness. The officer told me Bill had been taken to St. Vincent's Hospital. By the time I tracked down the doctor there, we'd gotten back to our house.

The doctor recommended that I come as soon as possible. I took the next available flight, thankful that Spokane to Portland was only forty-five minutes by air.

On the flight to Portland, I thought about how my subconscious had cast Bill in the role of my would-be protector. In a dream that I started having as a child and that had occasionally revisited me as an adult, Bill, our sister Diana, and I are grade-school-aged kids in the back seat of the family car. No one is in the front seat. The car is parked in front of our house. Although our street was flat, in my dream the car faces down a steep hill. The car begins to roll. Bill scrambles into the driver's seat and tries to steer. He is too short to see over the dashboard. His feet dangle helplessly far above the brake pedal. The car rolls faster and faster and faster. My stomach churns as I hug Diana, both of us crying. Then I wake up.

In real life, my brother had been my sometime nemesis. We had been latchkey kids before the term was invented. Being on our own after school made us feel grown up, though we didn't always act like it. One time Bill chased me through the house. I don't remember why, but I knew he'd make me regret it if he caught me. I saw my mother's car coming into the driveway and ran out of the house to tell her my side of the story first, knowing she'd take my side when she heard me out. The storm door swung back with so much force that when Bill put his arm out to stop it, the glass broke and sliced his wrist. Mom took him to the emergency room for stitches, leaving me to take care of Diana and sit with the guilt of my brother's blood. Within our family, the story was often repeated. *Remember the time when Carol made Bill cut his wrist because she'd broken the rule about running in the house?* Bill had the scar to prove it.

Our mother had been the glue holding the Miller family together. After Mom's death, that left just Bill and me. Diana had died of cancer three years before Mom, our dad twenty-seven years earlier.

My nod toward keeping the Miller remnant together consisted of arranging at least one meal with Bill whenever my husband and I were in Portland and calling him once a month. I'd time my call to catch him while he was having his morning coffee. I avoided calling after work, when our conversations would be punctuated with the rattle of ice as Bill lifted a glass to his lips, then lowered it. The sound conjured our father's tumblers of scotch—memories I wanted to avoid.

Bill's standard response to my "How are you doing?" was a bitter, "Oh, you know, living the dream." For twelve years, Bill had worked in the same auto body shop, doing alignments on cars after collision repairs. I heard a lot about his boss, whom he despised. The man was quick with blame and stingy with praise. Ever since Bill had filed a workers' compensation claim to cover the cost of his surgery for carpal tunnel syndrome, the guy had been trying to make Bill's life miserable enough that he would quit. It had been years since Bill had gotten a raise.

In spring and summer, Bill umpired adult recreational softball games in his spare time to make extra money. He'd often tell me about some guy giving him guff over a call he'd made. I pictured Bill going toe-to-toe with someone up in his face, staying calm while standing his ground.

I gathered that Bill's social life centered on the bar at Chan's, a place close to his apartment. I hoped its proximity improved the chances that he'd get home safely on nights when he had a few too many. When Bill had been diagnosed with sleep apnea, I'd wondered what proportion of his "sleep" was in fact drunken stupor. He'd gotten a CPAP machine, though he used it only sporadically. The CPAP was, he said, too much of a pain to clean.

More often recently, Bill recounted his latest trip to the hospital to receive a cardioversion treatment for his atrial fibrillation. Neither of us brought up that our father had died of a heart attack at sixty-one, an age that Bill was nearing.

As my plane descended into the Portland airport, I saw Mount Hood looking like a slightly crumpled magician's hat behind the city's fir-covered hills. Sighting the oft-hidden mountain failed to lift my mood.

For four days I sit holding Bill's hand during the short visits allowed in the cardiac ICU. I watch his chest move up and down. I listen to the relentless rhythm of the machines that breathe for him and keep the circulation going in his motionless legs. His bed is an island in a sea of linoleum in which boxy pieces of electronic equipment are scattered like icebergs. His diagnosis is multiple organ failure brought about by a cardiopulmonary crisis.

The only way to have a face-to-face conversation with Bill's medical staff is to be available to them whenever they are around. When not with Bill, I spend hours in the lobby outside the cardiac unit answering email on my laptop and talking with my assistant and deans on my cell phone. I take brief walks, doing a lap or two around the hospital's perimeter. Winding through the hospital's hallways,

I read the wall inscriptions about its founders, the Sisters of Providence. Though the place had evolved into a huge nonprofit corporation, they still laid claim to their founding mission of witnessing to Jesus by serving the poor and vulnerable. I watch other worried people, sad people, and bored people, all sitting in the lobby. Some of them are invited into a small room off the lobby. They come out weeping.

During one foray outside the hospital, I go over to Bill's apartment to retrieve his cell phone and make sure that things are turned off that need to be. This is my first time there. Each apartment in the three-story building has an external door opening directly onto the exposed walkway, like the motel where MLK was shot. I avoid touching the handrail as I climb the stairs.

The apartment's front door opens directly into the combination living room and dining area, with a kitchenette in the corner. A half-gallon bottle of Johnny Walker sits on the counter, two-thirds empty. Dirty dishes fill the sink. The place smells of dust tinged with mildew.

Bill had gotten rid of most of the decent furniture he owned when he'd moved in with a woman named Elenore a few years back. He'd met her through a Harley social media site. It had taken me years to tumble to the significance of his email address: "bigwilly." Bill was bragging about being generously endowed so he could attract biker babes. Elenore was not exactly a babe. She was an average-looking divorcee with a teenaged special-needs daughter named Ashley. And though Elenore liked riding second seat on Harleys, she spent weekdays cooking in a high-school cafeteria. I'd lost track of how many years they were together, but long enough that Elenore and Ashley were folded into our family celebrations, including my in-laws' sixtieth anniversary party. When they broke up, Bill cobbled together thrift store furnishings that make the large flatscreen TV and an imitation brass display case stand out. The glass shelves of the curio cabinet hold Bill's pool and racquetball trophies, along with memorabilia from when he'd owned a Texaco gas station dealership.

One of the few things hanging on the walls is a watercolor that I gave Bill in the mid-1990s. I'd spent ten days in China, on a conference junket financed by the Templeton Foundation. Just before my flight home I'd seen a stack of small, unframed original paintings on sale in the airport gift shop. I picked out half a dozen to give as Christmas gifts that year. The one I'd had matted and framed for Bill depicts bamboo shoots against a yellow background. "Lucky Bamboo," the tags on the sprigs sold in grocery-store florist sections claim. The picture is the closest thing to greenery Bill's place contains.

As I wash up the dishes, I consider pouring the liquor down the drain but decide to let it be. After taking out the trash, I throw clean underwear, socks, sweats, cell phone and charger, checkbook, laptop, and an address book that looks like it might have useful contact information and passwords into a box. During my hunt through his desk, I find a photo of Bill standing in the middle of a phalanx of bare-breasted Vegas showgirls, their height and stiletto heels bringing their jutting nipples to eye level for my five-foot-six brother. He looks perhaps twenty years younger, still in his Sonny Bono phase—luxuriant dark mustache, hair worn longish on the sides despite the slightly receding hairline. Back then, he really had been living his dreams. I put the photo back where I'd found it.

On my way to the parking lot, I retrieve Bill's mail and stop by the manager's office. I verify the address where the rent checks need to go and give the guy my phone number, asking him to, please, keep an eye on Bill's motorcycle.

The work my brother did as a gas station owner in his twenties required both manual skill and intellectual acumen. Bill loved the mix of management and hands-on auto repair, no two days ever exactly alike. Bill took pride in his trade.

A few years after Bill bought the station, a freeway upgrade closed the off-ramp that led to it for months. That put him into bankruptcy and sent him back to working for others as a mechanic. Later, when cars became computerized, general mechanics became like smithies—a relic of a bygone era. So, he'd become an alignment specialist. Doing alignments is skilled but repetitive work. Work that was hard on an aging body and corrosive to the spirit.

Simone Weil would not have been surprised that as my brother Bill's trade eroded into repetitive motion, his work eroded more than his body. Though she observes that when an apprentice gets hurt or tired, French workmen say, "It's the trade getting into his body," she held that physical labor is not in itself degrading. *Trade*, in its earliest usage, meant a habitual mode of life—a path that one treads. Later the word meant skilled manual labor and was contrasted with the professions. Weil admired the inherent usefulness of manual labor, while thinking that intellectual labor—especially abstract thought—needed to prove its worth.

In her mid-twenties, Weil caused her aristocratic parents' consternation by taking a job in a factory. They couldn't understand it, given that she was a top university graduate. But Weil, who was flirting with Marxism, wanted firsthand experience that would help her understand how industrial society could be reorganized to become less oppressive.

After a year of such work, she concluded that there was no such thing as a nonoppressive factory. The mindlessness of automated work, she thought, robs manual labor of its dignity. Weil's time in the factory shaped her writings on affliction. Though mindless repetitive labor might not cause affliction in every worker, it was one aspect of industrialization that made conditions rife for it, especially if the worker was laid low by sickness.

Doing alignments is not mindless work. But compared to the challenges of being a small business owner or a general-service auto mechanic, my brother Bill may well have found it degrading.

By day five, Bill's condition is unchanged. My husband and I have rooms booked at Lake McDonald in Glacier National Park for us, our two sons, and their wives. We plan to do some hiking and river rafting. This would be the first time we'd all been together since Steve and I moved from Michigan to Washington state over a year ago.

On the phone, Steve and I debate whether to rearrange our plans. Maybe he should go without me, so I won't be six hundred miles away when Bill might need me. But I miss my children. I choose to go. I say goodbye to Bill, not knowing whether he can hear me or whether it will be a last goodbye.

Once gone, I call the hospital twice a day for updates from the nurse. Less often, I succeed in conferring with one of the doctors. I need to stand in just the right spot near the shore of Lake McDonald to get cell phone reception. Dread hangs like a scrim between me and the light glinting off the water. On our hikes, I am half there, as half of me keeps distant vigil for Bill.

There's little change. Week one in the cardiac ICU turns into week two. At one point, a medical resident calls me for a decision about whether to administer a "clot buster" medication that may deal with Bill's crisis of the day. Without it he will likely die, but it also might precipitate a stroke. The drug works. That rarity, a third week in ICU, begins. After finishing our vacation, I get some urgent things done at work, then head back to Portland.

CHAPTER 2

Miracle Shake

As soon as I arrive back at the hospital on my second visit, I'm escorted into a conference room. Bill's attending doctor, a palliative care nurse, and a social worker all look serious and sad, in a professional, studied way. Their news is grim. As the sister—the only living relative—we need you to decide, they say. Your brother is conscious, but he is not going to get better. He can talk now that the breathing tube is out, but his communication is erratic. We don't think he understands his situation. His kidneys have failed; his liver is failing; his heart is in distress; his lungs are not good. His unstable blood pressure is making it hard to do dialysis effectively. If treatment continues, at best he'll be in a care facility for whatever time he has left. Would your brother want that? If we transition him to palliative care and stop dialysis, he will pass away peacefully within a few days.

I knew Bill, I thought. More than once Bill had said, "I hope I never have to be in a place like that," referring to the skilled nursing facilities our mother had needed on and off in the last year of her life. When Bill was a child he'd swagger around in a fake racoon-skin cap singing "Davey, Davey Crockett, king of the wild frontier" as loud as he could. As an adult who couldn't afford both a car and a motorcycle, he opted to ride his Harley-Davidson year-round. Like a great white shark, Bill would die without movement. Tearing up,

I say, "He would not want to linger unless there was some hope of getting back on his Harley."

All three of them look relieved. The social worker hands me tissues, saying I should go be with my brother now.

When I enter his room, Bill opens his eyes, looks straight at me and says, "It's about time." He looks at the ceiling, swallows, smacks his lips.

"What can I get for you?"

"A milkshake would taste real good."

I head out to find an ICU nurse. After a surprising amount of hunting, I find a large man who looks like a nightclub bouncer except that he's wearing scrubs. His name badge says "Danny." When I introduce myself and ask about a milkshake, he responds, "Ice chips. He can have ice chips. Nothing else by mouth. His swallow isn't reliable. We don't want him aspirating food into his lungs. Don't want him choking."

I go back and offer Bill some ice chips on a spoon. He takes one. Sucks on it. Waits. Opens his mouth for another. He looks exhausted by the effort to hold his head up.

"What day is it? How long have I been here?"

I fill him in on the timeline, looking for signs that he understands. Danny comes in, checks some of the monitors, and asks Bill how he is feeling. "I feel like crap," he says without making eye contact.

Another doctor, a stranger to me, comes in. He sits down and begins asking Bill questions. He is reading from a list: *What day is it? What month? Where are you? Do you understand why you are here?* Bill deflects many of the questions, others he answers sarcastically. As the doctor takes notes, I can see Bill's irritation. Being a smart-ass is his habitual mode of dealing with people who I would call officious. He'd call them assholes. The doctor excuses himself and leaves.

Bill asks, "How about that milkshake?"

"They say that's not a good idea. Ice chips are better."

"That's shitty."

"I can ask again."

Finding Danny, I explain that Bill would really like a milkshake. "If the doctors think that he will only live a few more days, what is the point of withholding the one thing that he wants?" Danny doesn't look happy, but he says he'll check.

After a while, Danny waves through the interior window for me to come out in the hallway and talk. "The doctor says a milkshake will be okay if you are very careful and take it slow."

Finding out that there is no such thing available in the hospital, I go to ask Bill what flavor he wants and tell l him I'll be back soon. At the McDonald's drive-through, I order a strawberry shake and ask for a spoon. By the time I return to Bill's room, he looks asleep, but his head turns in my direction, and he opens his eyes.

"Got it," I say, holding it up for him to admire. "Do you want some now?" He nods.

We gradually work our way through half the shake, one spoonful at a time. With his dentures removed and his uptilted, balding head, my brother looks like a baby bird waiting for a worm from his mother. His palpable enjoyment staves off my sense of haplessness.

As I drive to where I am staying, I ponder how to clear my calendar for the days or weeks that will be my brother's last. During my call with Steve, I am calm. Then I call my boss, Whitworth's president, to let him know I might be gone for quite a while. My voice breaks.

When I arrive the next morning in Bill's room, he is sitting up taller in bed. We talk quietly about how I've tried to keep his life afloat. Yes, I have talked with his boss, but the guy won't mail Bill's last paycheck, claiming Bill needs to pick it up in person. I tell Bill that Steve and I have paid his rent. I ask what other bills there are. Are they all coming automatically from his bank account, or do we need to send checks? The doctor who'd been one of the three-person group that met with me yesterday comes in.

"How are you feeling, Mr. Miller?"

"Better."

"That's good. Vitals are better. Early to say, but I am encouraged."

This more than surprises me. Isn't this the same doctor who yesterday explained why there was no point in further treatment? I ask for a few minutes to talk with him and follow him out of the room.

"So, you're saying that my brother will recover?"

"Blood pressure appears to have stabilized. That was our major concern. Your brother is still very, very sick, but he may gradually improve. The liver may recover. With the kidneys that is less likely. Mobility? Who knows? Cognitive deficits? Again, hard to know. But it looks like he will make it out of ICU to a regular hospital floor."

For the next few days, Bill and I joke about how much money he could get making testimonials for McDonald's shakes. *Miracle shake. Last wish turns into new lease on life.*

What I cannot say, even to myself, is that my dread has changed, not gone away. Keeping Bill comfortable and staying with him through his last days was one thing, getting Bill back to whatever his new normal will be is quite another. For weeks, I'd been dreading Bill's death, and, when I was not next to him, I had dreaded Bill's dying without me. Now that the future is literally unimaginable, what I dread is all the unknowable ways that Bill's future will be impossible without my sharing it.

Before returning to Spokane from the second trip to Portland, I make an appointment with the hospital social worker assigned to Bill's case. I want her advice about how to deal with what I foresee. I tell her, "I think my brother is an alcoholic and that he'll start drinking again as soon as he can."

She is unsurprised. She tells me they'd treated Bill for alcohol withdrawal during the first days in the ICU.

"So, what do you suggest I do?"

She tells me that adults have a right to folly, using the phrase as if it were a legal term. She says that if my brother choses to drink, knowing that he's continuing to undermine his now even more fragile health, there was nothing much I could do about it.

"You can't protect your brother from himself."

CHAPTER 3

Holey Safety Net

Looking back, I wonder how much time I would have eked out to help Bill if his health crisis hadn't started in the summer, when work was plentiful, but few matters were urgent. From September through May, my Whitworth University work started at my kitchen table at six in the morning and went until nine or ten at night. During the academic year, I caught up on emails from the day before while eating breakfast. These were usually a mix of questions, updates, requests, and complaints from faculty, students, and parents of students, as well as random people from off campus who thought they knew more than the bozos running the university. After breakfast, I would shower and walk to my campus office.

From 7:30 or 8 a.m. to 5 p.m., my days were filled with meetings—many with individuals, but most with the dozen standing committees I either chaired or was a member of. Those committee meetings constitute the university's nervous system. Routinely traversing Whitworth's neural pathways enabled me to foresee how my decisions would reverberate through the university and impact the work of others and, most importantly, the education of students.

The days were long, but some of my evening work was hardly work at all. I enjoyed both the artistry on display and the learning I gleaned from concerts, plays, and lectures. People noticed when the provost showed up—and when she didn't. My presence sent the signal that Whitworth's powers that be cared about what faculty and students were accomplishing.

A line from a children's book I read to my sons has stayed with me ever since. "Children were never bored in her classes," it said of some miraculous teacher. I am certain I bored many students over the years. But after escaping jobs like broccoli-packing, waitressing, and serving as a bank teller, I had enjoyed the privilege of doing work that never bored me. Some days I remembered to be appropriately grateful for that privilege. I think Bill felt that way about his work when he had been his own boss at the Texaco gas station. We were both problem-solvers who wanted things to work better. Bill tackled mechanical problems, I tackled ethical and organizational ones.

Once, the wife of one of my philosophy colleagues told me he had come home from a faculty meeting and asked her, "Have you ever seen Carol angry?" She reported replying, not that she could recall, to which he said, "Well, when she's angry, she stays very calm but clenches her jaw and talks very, very slowly, using small words, as if she thinks the person she is talking to is an imbecile." Hearing that was like catching a glimpse of my reflection on a bad hair day. As I entered the catch-22 world of applying for disability on Bill's behalf, I began having many bad hair days.

The first thing I found out is that there is no way to talk directly to a human being when calling Social Security—either their local office or their 1-800 number. I left multiple voicemail messages at Bill's local Social Security office. I knew that no one would try more than once to reach me, so I needed to be able to take their calls whenever they came. I found that by being persistent I could break through the endless menu of electronic voicemail options and eventually talk with a human being, but at no time in the process did I talk to the same human being twice.

When I finally got to talk to someone, she directed me to a website where I could access a form that seemed designed to be impossible to complete. When I found some of the questions mystifying and called the 1-800 number for advice, I got a voice message directing me back to the website or to my local Social Security office, which would direct me back to the website. At the end of the form, I had to sign something swearing that Bill was incapable of filling out the form himself.

That led to stage two of the process. The Social Security Administration sent me an appointment time for a phone interview. No one asked what times might work for me; they simply stipulated the day and time. There was no way of contacting someone to arrange an alternative time. I rearranged my calendar to be able to take the call. The caller re-asked the questions on the questionnaire.

The contrast between this runaround and the way Whitworth University handled family and medical leave situations infuriated me. Even before classes began during my first semester at Whitworth, a young international faculty member was hit in a crosswalk a mile from the campus by an inattentive driver. She had only been in the country for three weeks, had yet to teach a course for us, and had a severe closed-head injury. I worked with the head of Whitworth's human resources department to figure out how to negotiate this woman's visa situation as she began paid sick leave. Members of her department—people who had just started to get to know her—helped her make the transition from a rehabilitation center to living in the apartment that she'd only partially furnished before her accident.

Such early experiences of Whitworth's care for employees contrasted starkly with the callousness of Bill's former boss in withholding Bill's final paycheck. Like almost everyone I knew, I took paid sick leave for granted. Nothing in my life to that point had prepared me for the morass that desperately ill people without paid sick leave must navigate to obtain disability assistance.

At the end of her first year as a factory worker, Simone Weil says that it would have been better to have been whipped than to have had to repress all that was best in herself. The nature of the work exhausted her and exacerbated her chronic migraines, leaving her unable to think. But for her, the most tortuous job requirement was deference to arbitrary authority. She saw that the demand for deference created a kind of docility in the workers that struck her as akin to slavery.

Now I was experiencing firsthand how deference to arbitrary authority characterized not just the work life of those in the working class, but their disability as well. Bill was spared these indignities, at least for the present, because he was spending most of his time sleeping. When awake, he inched toward recovering the ability to do the simplest bodily tasks without assistance.

Part of the hostility I experienced from Social Security employees likely stemmed from people's dislike for being talked to as if they were imbeciles. But eventually, I did get to stage three of the process, which was Social Security setting a time for a phone interview with Bill. Fortunately, by then he had recovered the strength to hold a cell phone.

More than a month of this runaround resulted in Bill's application being approved. Great news. The less-than-good news was that his disability payments would not start until six months after his last day of paid employment. Bill might be dead by then, but he also might be back in his apartment—if he still had an apartment.

Social Security is our society's social safety net, intended to prevent poverty among the aged and keep disabled people from becoming homeless. In the case of the disabled, the price of accessing that safety net is steep. I encountered rudeness, indifference, condescension, dismissal, disregard, contempt, and suspicion from its gatekeepers. I suspected that the problem was systemic, caused not by hiring callous bunglers but by turning once-decent people into drones of bureaucratic regulations and hyperdocumentation. People doing repetitive work, corrosive to the soul.

My third trip to Portland since Bill almost died is timed to help with Bill's transition to a rehabilitation center. During the six weeks that Bill has been in the hospital, he has shifted from needing daily dialysis to needing it only three days a week. He's moved from a semi-liquid diet to soft foods to regular foods. He's progressed from needing someone to hold the phone for him while he talks to being able to initiate calls on his cell phone. His liver function has improved. But his breathing remains labored and wheezy, and he's made slow progress on walking, in part because his feet are so swollen that his shoes no longer fit. So far, dialysis is not keeping up with his fluid retention.

Though Bill is well enough to leave the hospital, it is too early to tell when or if he will be able to live on his own. Steve and I are continuing to pay his rent, not because we think he'll be able to return to his apartment, but because we're unwilling to let go of this concrete, dismal hope. The apartment is a dump, but, to Bill, it's home.

The morning Bill will be discharged, I accompany him to his last inpatient dialysis treatment, walking beside his wheelchair as the hospital attendant pushes him down the hallway. The room we enter has four recliners sitting next to large machines. Two chairs are already occupied. As attendants get Bill situated, I introduce myself to the nephrologist and ask if it is okay for me to sit with Bill during the treatment.

"Okay with me," she says, shrugging. Once during the treatment, she comes over to talk with Bill. She looks at the two of us and says, "No mistaking that she's your sister."

She parries Bill's barbed comments with New Jersey–accented jibes. I can tell that Bill likes her. He soon seems to be dozing off. I take a book out of my bag and try to read.

When Bill and I get to his rehab center later that day, we see few people in its wide hallways. Open doors to the rooms we pass reveal slack-jawed residents, some in bed with eyes aimed at blaring TVs, some slumped in wheelchairs. Most residents look twenty years older than Bill. Most staff look thirty to forty years younger. The only things recommending this place are an available bed and its acceptance of Medicaid, in which the hospital had enrolled Bill on the second day of his hospital stay. Because he already owed them money from previous uses of their emergency room, the hospital knew that he was uninsured. Over the years, Bill's boss had eliminated his paid vacation, then his paid sick leave, then employer contributions to medical insurance. Bill had decided to drop his insurance and bet that his out-of-pocket costs would be less than his insurance payments. He had long ago lost that bet.

There's an amputee in the other bed in Bill's double room. The stump on his leg sticks out from the rumpled sheets as he watches a game show on the wall-mounted TV. I help Bill out of the wheelchair to the edge of his bed, where he perches, panting.

My brother has not had a haircut in over six weeks, so I get out the buzzer I'd retrieved from his apartment and neaten up the fringe around his bald crown. As I sort through what he's brought from the hospital, I find a fat box set of booklets about living with kidney failure. *Dialysis Diet. Psychological Health During Treatment. What Your Family Should Know.*

"Have you read these?" I ask.

"Nope. Don't plan to."

Later, while Bill dozes, I read the booklets—learning that he should avoid cheese, potatoes, and salt. He should restrict fluids—not just beverages, but soups, sauces, and most fruits. The diet booklet recommends sucking on a frozen grape as a strategy for coping with thirst. Bill loves to eat. Virtually everything he likes is on the restricted list. The booklet on psychological health warns that fatigue and depression are common in people with renal failure. Its ending is trite: "Many dialysis patients learn how to live normal, happy lives."

Though Bill never read those booklets, he did take time to read his eighty-page medical record from the hospital. Though he had had no control over what he'd been put through, he wanted to understand it. I know that because more than once he said, "My sister told them to pull the plug on me," giving me a sideways glace. My agreement to the discontinuation of his dialysis after three weeks in ICU had been noted on his chart. Bill aimed most of his bitterness about how close he had come to dying at his attending ICU doctor, but there was plenty left over for what he saw as my complicity.

His chart also noted that I'd used the term *alcoholic* when talking with his social worker. He was ticked, thinking I'd been out of line. "I'm no alcoholic," he insisted.

One plus of having made a successful application for disability was that Bill now had a single person at his local Social Security office assigned to his case. When I called, I could now ask for Ellen. While seldom available on the first call, Ellen often called me back within a day or two.

"So, Ellen, help me understand how my brother is supposed to eat and pay his rent for another few months without any income and with no disability payments."

"Well, he can apply for SSI."

"What's SSI?"

"Supplemental Security Insurance. Does your brother have more than $2,000 in assets?"

"He has less than $200 in the bank. He has some dumpy furniture. He has a motorcycle."

"He's allowed one vehicle that won't be counted as an asset."

"So, I guess he qualifies."

"Great. You can find the application form online at ssa.gov."

So, I filled out the SSI application and eventually they scheduled a phone interview with Bill. The appointed time was on the second day after he had been discharged from the hospital. I wheeled him out into the courtyard of his rehab facility so that he'd have a quiet place to take the call. I sat on a bench across from him and saw emotions come and go on his face: concentration, puzzlement, irritation. "Yes," he said multiple times between long pauses to listen. "No," he said, after others. At one point he looked over at me and asked, "What's the address here?"

"Why?"

"They are asking for the address where I live."

I looked the address up on my cell phone and read it to him slowly, pausing as he repeated each part of it into his phone.

A few days later, I received a notification that his claim had been denied because he did not need assistance with living expenses. The reason given was that he was not living in his home.

As a listener of National Public Radio, I had repeatedly heard the tagline of one of their sponsors, the Melville Charitable Trust: "Finding and fighting the causes of homelessness." I now knew that being a blue-collar worker without paid sick leave who is too sick to navigate the Social Security system must be high on that list. I cringe for others in medical circumstances similar to Bill's, who, having no one to pay their rent, would have been evicted long before they got out of the hospital. I picture them—physically weak, disoriented, and the process of applying for disability still looming ahead of them—suddenly discovering that the contents of their former apartment are long gone and that they have no place to go but a homeless shelter. How could they escape being numbered among the afflicted?

I filed an appeal of Bill's disability denial with Social Security. I strove to maintain a respectful tone as I stated the obvious point: Although Bill was temporarily in a rehab center, his rent needed to be paid so he'd have a place to live when he was discharged.

CHAPTER 4

Under the Rubble

The day after his SSI interview, I accompanied Bill to his first outpatient dialysis treatment. I followed his prearranged, mass transit handicapped transport in my rental car. Before I could go in with Bill, the receptionist made me sign a waiver form stating that I knew the risks of blood-borne pathogens. She had me put a hospital gown with long puffy sleeves on over my street clothes.

As we entered a large room, I saw dozens of recliners in rows. I'd been expecting something more like the four-station inpatient dialysis room at the hospital. Instead, the place looked like a mammoth pedicure salon, except for the fact that there were large machines sitting next to each recliner.

An attendant wheeled Bill to one of the recliners and I helped him transition to the chair. An attendant came with a clipboard to verify his information and asked him to sign forms. Eventually another attendant came to hook up tubes from the hemodialyzers to the port that's lodged near his clavicle. This had become a familiar ritual to my brother from many weeks of inpatient treatment, but I was seeing it for only the second time.

"This'll take about four hours," the attendant said, looking over at me. He finished and walked away. During those four hours, my brother's blood would be extracted from his body, pumped through filters, then returned. The goal was that he'd end up with less fluid, fewer toxins, and balanced electrolytes. Removing too much fluid would cause painful cramping. Taking too little would stress his heart and lungs. No matter how well the process went, Bill always felt like he'd run a hilly road race. Sometimes he felt like he'd been pummeled along the way.

Bill had said almost nothing since we arrived. As he inserted his earbuds to listen to iTunes, I scanned the room, watching the staff and trying to guess their roles. I wondered about the stories of the other patients in the chairs. The place had the bustle and passivity of a bus terminal, an atmosphere poised on the cusp of hope and despair. I noticed that unlike me, none of those getting treatment wore a protective gown. I wondered who decided that it was less important that they were protected from blood-borne pathogens than visitors or staff.

A perky thirty-year-old came by and introduced herself as one of the center's social workers. She said she'd help Bill apply for extra assistance from the American Kidney Foundation. I asked to be able to talk with her when she had a minute. Bill closed his eyes and looked like he'd try to nap. The social worker and I went out into the lobby.

I said, "I have a few questions. Also, there are some things it might be helpful for you to know. My brother will not be a compliant patient. What will happen if he doesn't eat the way he should? He also drinks. He's likely to start that again if he gets back to his own place. How bad will that be for him?"

"We are used to people not cooperating fully. The more liquid he consumes beyond the recommended amount, the more he'll cramp up during dialysis. Over time many people get the hang of what their body needs."

"How long can he survive on dialysis?"

"That varies. Many people do this for years. Some continue to work while on dialysis. They come in for dialysis at night. We do two sets of three shifts—early, midday and night, either Monday-Wednesday-Friday or Tuesday-Thursday-Saturday. Some people get set up to do dialysis at home. Bill might want to consider getting on the transplant list."

"I had no idea there were so many people who needed dialysis."

"Lots of different stories there. Congenital kidney failure. Diabetes. Infections. Injuries. Those are the main causes. Other diseases."

I checked back in with Bill and sat with him, trying to think of what to talk about in this public place. I thought I was used to the silence of Miller men. When I was young, our dad and I were often the first ones up, though he would have bested me by at least an hour. I started drinking coffee in my early teens, so we could sip in silence together on those mornings when he was not nursing a beer. That had felt companionable, but now Bill's and my silence crackled. I stood up, saying that I was going to buy him some new sweatpants and bedroom slippers with nonskid soles that would fit. I'd be back well before his treatment was finished.

I'd been inside the dialysis center for less than an hour. I felt depleted. To me, Bill's new normal felt like a torturous slow slide toward death. Bill would tell me little about how it felt to him.

Simone Weil admired Charlie Chaplin's *Modern Times*. The film is a dark comedy set in a factory. In one of its scenes, Chaplin emerges, manic, after being sucked into a machine's cog system. He is unable to keep his wrenches off anything boltlike, including the noses of his coworkers. In another scene, Chaplin sees a coworker sucked into a machine and tries to extricate the man. When the break whistle blows, Chaplin pauses his efforts. Only the man's head is visible as Chaplin sits beside him, calmly eating. Weil's most chilling description of affliction compares it to "a worker who has been pulled into the cogs of a machine. He is nothing more than a torn and bloodied thing." Real affliction uproots a person's life by damaging all its parts.

All affliction involves social degradation, or the fear of it, in some form or another. Weil tells us that the line between suffering and sorrow (however deep, violent, and lasting) and affliction is like the boiling point of water. The frog in the proverbial pot goes from comfortable to incapacitated without ever knowing it's cooked. Thus too, affliction sneaks up on its victims. Whether or not being wrung through the social-services wringer had made Bill feel as if he'd been sucked into a machine, being hooked to a dialyzer three times a week was bound to.

After returning home, I called daily to see how Bill was doing. "Oh, living the dream," he would often say.

In what amounts to an aside in his account of being a reconnaissance pilot during World War II, Antoine de Saint-Exupéry tells of having seen a man being pulled from a collapsed house's cellar after being trapped for many days. Those who excavated him kept asking how he'd felt. What they wanted to understand was: *Who were you? Who surged up in you?* The man kept giving unhelpful answers: *My back hurt quite a bit. I was worried about my watch.* The lesson that de Saint-Exupéry draws from his story is, "No single event can awaken within us a stranger totally unknown to us. To live is to be slowly born."

My daily calls to Bill seemed like the tapping a would-be rescuer might do. She hopes she's reassuring the person trapped under the rubble. *I'm not giving up. Neither should you.* She hopes that's what he's hearing. But the rescuer cannot know what it's like to be under the rubble.

Most of our daily phone calls were brief. Bill would be tired, and I would usually be on my way from one meeting to another. Much of what I heard from Bill were complaints. The food was bad. His roommate was loud. His physical therapist had again shown up right after he'd returned from dialysis, when he'd been too tired to move. He'd told her to come later, but she never did. He had to wait over an hour—again—to be picked up from the dialysis center. Complaining came naturally to Bill and, goodness knows, he had plenty of grounds for it now. He felt like a hostage to others' incompetence.

Then one day, Bill sounded happy when I called. "Something good happened today," he said. "I helped somebody." He told me about a woman in a room down the hall from him who had been having an awful day and who he'd been able to listen to and comfort. "I think I did her some good." He sounded proud. That had not surged up in Bill out of nowhere. What had surged up was the opportunity and the energy to get himself up and down the hallway—to act and not just be acted upon by the "machine" of Medicaid-funded rehabilitation. Pride in being useful was as natural to him as complaint. That day gave me hope that he'd begun to emerge from the rubble of his life.

Twelve weeks after being transported to the hospital in an ambulance, Bill returned to his apartment. He'd spent six weeks in the limbo of that rehab center. As someone who has had a lifetime of good health, I cannot fathom how my brother survived during that time. Bill's life had not been luxurious before it caved in. It would never be completely restored.

When Bill first transitioned home, Medicaid paid for a visiting nurse, a shower aide, transportation to outpatient dialysis, and some minimal housekeeping for him. So far as his needs were medical, the system gave him adequate support.

SSI, which we had finally secured four months after Bill's ambulance ride to the hospital, paid enough to cover his rent. Meals on Wheels delivered one meal a day to supplement the food with which I had stocked his kitchen in preparation for his move home. Two months later, Social Security started his disability payments, which were just enough to disqualify him for Medicaid. As he transitioned to Medicare, he began to be charged copays for services that Medicaid had provided for free.

Several weeks after his return home, Bill's doctor signed off on his ability to drive. That was fabulous news, but Bill had no car and far too little muscle tone to handle his Harley safely. Without a car, he was housebound unless he used Dial-a-Ride or had a friend take him somewhere. His frustrations about this came up frequently when we talked.

Bill's friends were a less frequent topic of conversation. Pete, a longtime friend who used to be Bill's racquetball partner, would pick

Bill up on Saturdays and take him to breakfast. I'd never met Pete and didn't know what he did for a living, but more than once he'd helped Bill debug his computer.

Other friends, Robin and Rachel, had visited Bill in the rehab center. Whenever Bill mentioned them, I pictured a tragicomic rescue. Years before, the two of them had been boating with Robin's father and their boat had sunk. Robin was the strongest swimmer among them and had had to choose whom to help first to shore. He had chosen his father, thinking that Rachel would be able to make it on her own. By the time he'd gone back for Rachel, she had been underwater for a while. He did CPR on her until the EMTs arrived, but she spent several weeks in a coma before recovering. Even though Robin had swum his father to shore first, his father ended up dying. I met Robin and Rachel when they came to our mother's memorial service. Rachel said that she'd always been grateful for my mother's prayers on her behalf.

Bill soon got weary of having to ask Pete or Robin or Rachel for rides. And I got weary of hearing him complain about Dial-a-Ride. Steve and I had a Chevrolet Malibu that we'd bought used before we left Michigan. We also had a Honda CR-V that we'd bought shortly after arriving in Spokane, thinking we needed its four-wheel drive on Spokane's hills in the winter. Some days, both cars sat in our driveway all day since I walked to Whitworth most days and Steve had yet to find work. We decided to lend Bill our Malibu until he could get back on the Harley—or sell it and get a car of his own.

The Malibu boosted his morale. Providing one small step toward a normal life for my brother boosted my morale as well. Bill felt well enough by Thanksgiving to drive himself across Portland to join us for the holiday buffet at The Springs, the senior living center where Steve's mother lived. Bill drank two glasses of wine and topped off his dinner off with two slices of pie. Watching him eat, I remembered how often our father had urged us to get our money's worth when he took us to an all-you-can-eat buffet.

Another large step toward Bill's new normal was surgery on his arm to build a fistula. I had only a vague idea of what this was but knew that it replaced the plastic access that had been lodged near Bill's clavicle for months. "Not exactly a chick magnet," Bill had snarked the first time I'd seen it. Saying good riddance to it buoyed him for a while, until his frustration grew over having needles directly poked into the fistula in his arm three times a week.

During the months when Bill was literally in abject need, my path seemed simple. Do what is needed, spend whatever that cost. The costs were ones Steve and I could easily bear. But once Bill was back in charge of his own finances, I found the dynamic set up by our pasts confusing.

Years ago, soon after our mother's death, Bill asked me to loan him $2,000, which at that point in Steve's and my financial life was a startling amount of money. We had more than that in savings, but we also had two young sons and college for them looming down the road. I knew that both Bill and Diana had borrowed money from Mom at various times, which bothered me, especially after she stopped working and had little beyond Social Security to live on. I knew that they both bought impulsively, enticed by "easy monthly installments." I knew from sorting through Diana's bills when she was dying, that when she maxed out one credit card, she applied for another. She picked which bills to pay each month and which to defer. I guessed that Bill did the same. I expected that, if I lent Bill that money, he would indeed eventually pay it back. I also suspected that, not long after he paid it back, he'd be asking for another loan.

I discussed Bill's request with Steve and together we decided we would send Bill $900, an amount we thought we could afford, but I would emphasize that it was a gift. "I don't loan money to family," I told him. In all the years after that, Bill never again explicitly asked me for money. Once Steve and I reached a point where we had real discretionary income, I sent Bill a check for a couple of hundred dollars for his birthday and Christmas. Noblesse oblige it may have looked like to Bill—perhaps welcome as cash but resented as a symbol of our differing social status.

My having drawn that line with Bill back then created complications. I now often worried that he was doing without things he genuinely needed. But I was flummoxed by the quandary of how to help someone who might forgo filling prescriptions for himself because he couldn't afford the copays, but who bought himself a Keurig and an Instant Pot.

Meanwhile, my calls to Bill continued to feel like tapping on a pile of suffering I only dimly understood.

CHAPTER 5

More than Cautionary Tales

In June of 2015, I needed to fly to Portland just for the day to connect with a grant officer. His foundation had been generous to Whitworth University, and it was part of my job to ensure that generosity continued. I called Bill, saying that I'd take an early flight if he wanted to get together for breakfast before my meeting. He suggested a place I'd never heard of, though it was on Halsey Street, a multilane arterial near the house where we grew up.

As I pulled my rental car into the parking lot, I realized that the diner sat across a side street from our childhood church. Our sister Diana had one of her weddings there, though by then our family had moved away a decade earlier. Bill had walked Diana down the aisle, as our father had been dead less than a year.

Looking over at the church, I remembered the backlit cross that hung in the recessed space above a tank that was hidden from those sitting in the sanctuary by a blank partial wall. When filled with water, the tank became the scene of the drama of immersion. During baptisms, the witnessing congregation could see just the upper half of the preacher and the person to be baptized—or, in the case of a child, her head and shoulders. As I waded into that tank at age eight, the water resisted my efforts to keep the white cotton shift I'd been given to wear from floating up and exposing my underpants. I remember envying Bill, who was being baptized in the same service, for being able to wear trousers and a white shirt. The preacher said, "I baptize thee in the name of the Father, the Son, and the Holy Ghost," while holding a handkerchief over my nose and mouth and bending me backward under the water. I came up sputtering.

I sat in my car wondering why Bill had picked this location. I doubted that he was nostalgic about Woodland Park Baptist. A few years after his baptism, Bill followed Dad's example of going to church once or twice a year at most.

As I got out of my car, Bill pulled in. I waited for him to leverage himself out of the driver's seat. He was wearing a Hawaiian shirt. Its deep blue suited him. He'd grown his goatee into a full beard, which was neatly trimmed. It had been a year since his initial health crisis. He'd put on weight. Although he looked stronger, he still walked like he was picking his way across a patch of ice.

We walked slowly toward the restaurant, which had an odd sort of mountain range roofline with a shoebox-shaped, plate-glass protrusion in the front. I dimly remembered the ground where we were standing as a vacant lot.

"How long has this place been here?" I asked.

"I don't know," he said shrugging. "Early seventies, maybe. They're supposed to have the best breakfasts on the east side. Barack Obama ate here when he was campaigning. They've got a picture of him schmoozing people hanging on the wall."

"Really? I used his book, *Dreams from My Father*, a few times in a course I taught." My imagination placed Obama in Hawaii, Chicago, and DC. Odd to think he'd been here, where we'd known only one Black family. Mr. Flowers coached Bill's Little League team. His son was the starting pitcher, Bill the catcher. I paused to look at the photo of Obama with two white guys. The man sitting next to Obama had a walrus mustache above his mouth's tight line. Obama had his arm extended toward the man sitting across from him. With his head turned away from the camera, there was no telling whether the guy was buying whatever Obama was saying.

As we slid into a booth, I got out my phone to show Bill the latest pictures of my granddaughter. I'd called him the day after she was born the February before. "They named her Riley Quinn," I said. "Matt and Julie said they liked the way it sounds. Sounds like someone who writes mystery novels."

"Yah, maybe," was all Bill said.

Bill showed little interest in the pictures of Riley. He looked out through the window and nodded. "Do you remember that the paper shack was just over there across Halsey? Back before they widened it." I remembered the building, but not its location. Unlike the church, the long-gone paper shack had tendrils in my brother. Bill's mentioning it called up cold Sunday mornings kneeling on the shack's wooden floor. Diana and I had helped Bill stuff the newspapers with the advertising inserts, folding and rubber-banding them for delivery, and putting them in plastic wrappers if the weather was wet. Mom drove us around, stopping every block or so. We'd each exit through a different car door, spreading out to toss papers on porches. There'd be time for hot chocolate at home before getting ready for church.

Bill must have been ten when he got his first paper route, which on weekdays he'd do by himself on his bike. Within a year, he earned his first trip to Disneyland by hustling up the needed number of new subscribers. To Diana and me, that seemed like a trip to the moon.

Bill saved the proceeds from his earnings to buy a better bike, which took him all over the east side of Portland. He'd come back with stories of riding up to Rocky Butte or down to the Columbia River, places Diana and I had to wait to be driven to by Mom or Dad.

Early on, Bill and I had been a pair. I, the adoring younger sister, joined him to catch grasshoppers in the long grass in a vacant lot down the block, scoop tadpoles from a nearby creek, or joust, using fallen branches, with a larger group of kids in a vacant lot two blocks from our house. At some point during grade school that changed. Having a girl in tow cramped his style. Diana and I then became a pair, spending a lot of time with two sisters down the block who, unlike us, had a swing set.

Our three-bedroom house on Sacramento Street looked like every other cracker box house on our treeless block. The houses varied only in color and in flipping which side held the bedroom windows and which held the living room's picture window. Our childhood had been as undistinguished as the suburb we lived in. As a child, I saw my family as unexceptional. Did our parents fight more than others? When you live on a narrow lot in a house without air conditioning, you hear many family arguments, not all of them your own.

As kids, one of our favorite fast-food places sold sandwiches called Satellite Burgers. Shaped like flying saucers, they were filled with ground beef, shredded lettuce, and special sauce. On warm evenings, we ate them sitting at one of the picnic tables near a creek that ran across one corner of the lawns behind the building. Large willows grew along the creek's banks. We kids ate quickly so we could chase the white ducks that waddled around begging for food while Dad and Mom finished eating.

One evening Mom took us to the Satellite Burger place. She waited until we were finished eating before saying that she had something she needed to tell us. She said that she and Dad were not going to be living together anymore. How old was I? Seven? Nine? I remember tears, the evening light, the weight in my stomach, the wrongness of having eaten.

Mom and Dad stayed together. I do not know what pushed my mother to the brink, or what pulled her back. Did our upset dissuade her? I do not want that heavy weight on the narrow, heaving shoulders of my young self. Perhaps the practical details of separation, when it came to it, proved more daunting than muddling along. Perhaps Mom's resolve to leave moved Dad toward one of his stints in rehab. So many unknowns.

Though our parents' marriage remained officially intact, loneliness curled up in its core. By the time I was in high school, they had given up sleeping in the same bedroom, even in twin beds. My father slept in their bedroom. My mother slept in her recliner—for the sake of her back and to keep her legs elevated, or so she said.

Our father was raised on Colorado's high eastern plains during the Dust Bowl. He grew into a man whose feelings outstripped his expressive powers. Being with him taught me to hear the intimations of sighs, to watch for the upturned corner of a mouth and the slight contraction of a muscle in a jaw or near the eyes.

Dad was a lumber buyer for a branch of a chemical company that treated logs with preservatives, then sold them as telephone poles and pilings for piers. Dad did most of his work in an office in downtown Portland. Sometimes on Saturdays he would take us kids there. We would go up the elevator with its brass trim to the hushed hallway. Our feet would echo on the corridor's marble floor as we passed doors with darkened, frosted windows. Though the office area held multiple shiny wooden desks, we never met anyone else who worked there. We kids took turns punching the keys and pulling the levers of a large, multirowed contraption. Meanwhile, Dad did whatever he did, his work as mysterious as the innards and point of the gunmetal-gray Monroe calculator.

Perhaps my memory mistakenly extrapolates the emptiness of his office space into a hollow work life. He talked more than once about disappointment with how his company treated him. Ever since reading Arthur Miller's *Death of a Salesman* for the first time in high school, I have seen my father as Willy Loman, a man whose loyalty to his firm was not repaid in kind. I have known many people like my father, who worked at their jobs because they happened into them and stayed. Work was something to do well enough to satisfy the boss. Pleasure came, if it came at all, from raises, promotions, weekends, and vacations.

Dad would come home tired and brooding, and drink tumblers of scotch and water—unless he was on the wagon. When Dad was off the wagon, he would have a beer with his coffee in lieu of breakfast—"hair of the dog" for his hangover.

One night he arrived in the middle of a family dinner. The food we were eating had already been kept warm too long by the time Mom decided to give up waiting and start without him. He walked unsteadily to the table. We kids kept our eyes on our plates as he asked, "Doesn't anyone have anything to say? What is this slop?" I picked at my food in silence until we were excused.

Dad never hit us, though he did kick the dog once in irritation. And his stretches of being on the wagon were longer and more frequent than being off. Still, the off times colored all other times with dread. He was a sad drunk, whose drinking made my mother sad and put the rest of us on high alert. I suspect he was also sadly sober, resenting that his disposition barred him from what, for others, was a normal part of socializing—unless they were Baptists.

Mom grew up in tiny Tustin, Michigan, where her father's livery business failed because of the rise of the automobile. As a young adult, Vera had been an office worker in the.auto industry in Flint. Growing up where Henry Ford began manufacturing the Model-T had imbued being behind the wheel with a romantic aura. Bill had caught that from her.

Often on a Sunday afternoon when we were young, after the dinner dishes were done and Dad was watching the San Francisco Giants on TV, she'd gather us kids into the car. She'd set off in a direction that we hadn't headed lately, with no definite destination in mind. She'd follow winding roads up into the hills surrounding Portland until we'd say, "Can we stop?" Then she'd pull into some little place that served warm donuts or pie. We never went home the same way we'd come. If we ever worried that we were lost, she'd say that, no, we'd just found an unexpected place. I learned early on not to underestimate my mother, though (much to my shame) I was often ashamed of her. During my lifetime, she was never less than a hundred pounds overweight, though she tried every slimming fad from Metrecal meal-replacement shakes to the grapefruit diet.

Mom was the church treasurer, a role that was a natural fit for her since she had worked as a bookkeeper most of her life. She was at the church almost as much as the pastor. After Bill stopped going to church, Diana and I played in the deserted church basement while my mother was in her meetings. I learned to associate church with waiting.

Mom suffered from chronic back pain and blood clots in her legs. Each time she developed a clot, she took blood thinners and spent several days with her leg elevated and a heating pad on it. Because of Mom's physical problems, from the time I was twelve, my sister and I did the house cleaning and cooked our family dinners.

Bill did no chores, because his paper route meant he needed no allowance, but also because he was a boy. By this time, Bill's presence in the house was an empty, messy bedroom—a room I entered only to place his clean laundry on his unmade bed. Which did I resent more: his not having to do his share around the house, or his not being around?

Mom's spurts of dieting and Dad's stretches of sobriety roughly coincided. During times of greatest tension between them, Mom gained extra weight. After teaching myself to sew in middle school, I modified the largest women's patterns I could find at the fabric store, adding extra material so that the resulting dresses would fit my mother. For both my parents, excess alternated with deprivation. Moderation was a rarity.

While in high school, Bill worked at a gas station after school and on weekends. He earned enough to buy himself a car, a used yellow Corvette Stingray, which he totaled the night of his high school graduation party. As far as I can recollect, he was uninjured. He replaced the Stingray with another, whose color has faded from my memory.

In my senior year of high school, I took a literature course in which my teacher assigned excerpts from Plato's *Republic*. One selection we read contained an allegory that Plato gives for the soul. Our souls, Plato claims, behave as if they are composed of three parts: one resembling a many-headed monster, one a lion, and one a man. The many-headed monster, unless it is held in check, will torment the lion, devour the man, and pull us willy-nilly in opposing directions. Plato claimed that when reason (the man) becomes wise enough to tame our will (the lion) and enlist its aid in pacifying our unruly desires (the monster), our violent internal chaos is transformed into harmony. Philosophy, the love of wisdom, thus brings peace to our souls.

My parents' struggles with their appetites for food and drink, my brother's appetite for fast cars, and the conflicts among my own adolescent desires, made Plato's psychology compelling. Reason's promise to provide internal harmony as well as external guidance partly explains my attraction to philosophy. But that is far from the whole story, just as my family members' lives are more than cautionary tales.

Three children of the same good-enough parents—parents whose equal pride in each of us never felt hard to earn. Bill was always the most competitive of us, Diana was most the performer, and I the most earnest. I needed my earnestness as protective gear. In grade school, I was one of those students who had to leave her main classroom for what we kids called "MR reading." "MR" stood for mentally retarded. You feel slightly less dumb when you are with other kids who also struggle, but you must do the walk of shame in returning to your classroom, everyone looking at you and knowing where you've been.

In middle school, my earnestness kept me striving for fewer words circled in red by my teachers—kept me sitting at the dining room table in the evening with a dictionary, my parents having said, "Look it up," whenever I asked how to spell something. Doing your homework takes a long time when your first, second, third, and fourth guess about a spelling are all still not correct, and you lose track of what word you're looking for because you find so many unknown words in the dictionary that you stop to read about.

Does what my dyslexia taught me about delayed gratification explain why I fared differently from my siblings? God only knows. But my parents' persistent confidence that I could handle any challenge goes a long way toward explaining why I did. And in hindsight, I see that my upbringing was a primer in the art of straddling. I was the daughter who was equally as willing to sip scorched percolator coffee with her silent dad as to wait in the church basement for her mom to finish the meetings that provided an escape from my father's remoteness. Loving my parents taught me to hold together remnants from rips I could not mend.

Though Bill's upbringing was in some sense the same as mine, it was importantly modulated by differences of birth order, gender, and reception. What was Bill's upbringing a primer for? That's a question I'm ill-equipped to answer. But, like many men of his generation, his upbringing did not equip him to cope well when his hard work was swamped by shifting contexts and he was made to feel obsolete.

Bill, Diana, and I were all first-generation college students—a phrase I did not hear until I was more than a decade into my faculty career. When I started college, the fact that your parents had not gone to college was unremarkable. It never occurred to me to think of it as a handicap. My father had gotten three $2,000 whole-life insurance policies when his children were babies, one to cash out for each child to provide for our advanced education. That was close to enough, back then, to cover four years of tuition at a public university. Each of the Miller children, in turn, enrolled at Portland State University after graduating from high school.

I do not know if Bill and Diana found their experience at Portland State as isolating as I did my first year. I rode the Tri-Met bus to class; I read; I studied; I talked with professors during office hours. My Baptist church taught me to view the university as a dangerous place full of false teaching. When I mentioned being interested in philosophy, well-meaning church members quoted the warning in the second chapter of Colossians about the deceitfulness of philosophy and prayed for my soul. My first philosophy professor played into this stereotype by announcing early in the course that he hoped there were no Jesus freaks in the room. Despite the snide comments of the professor, I found the course fascinating.

Bill and I were in that same Introduction to Philosophy class, which would have been my first term and the beginning of his second year. He did as well in the class as I did but liked it less. He must have been taking it to fulfill a humanities requirement. His major was law enforcement.

Unlike me, Bill had moved out of our parents' house after graduation and was working full-time as an auto mechanic while being a full-time student. Soon after we had that philosophy course together, Bill dropped out, setting aside his dream of becoming a policeman. Diana only made it through two terms before deciding to look for a full-time job. Because all three of us had inherited our father's reticence, I know as little about why they quit as they knew about why I kept going, even after stopping out of college for a year when I was nineteen to get married.

During Simone Weil's stints of manual labor, various trades—farming, fishing, manufacturing—got into her body in different ways. Simone Weil speaks of the scars she acquired placing metal parts into a factory furnace. She describes rising in anguish in the morning, and going to bed exhausted yet anxious over whether she'd sleep well enough to survive the next day's work.

The year I stopped out of college, I worked at a Birds Eye processing plant. Unlike Weil, I wasn't there in solidarity with the workers. I was there because, being a union shop, Birds Eye paid better than any other short-term job I could have gotten. For six months, I spent nine hours a day, six days a week packing blanched broccoli into small cartons that would be flash frozen for sale in grocery stores. Six months was not long enough for the trade to have gotten into my body, but the stench of tons of broccoli had gotten into my boots. There is no joy on earth like throwing your reeking work boots into the garbage the day you're done working at Birds Eye.

I would see my brother Bill die with car grease embedded in his finger pads and cuticles, though it had been years since he'd been physically able to labor in an auto repair bay. Other ways that Bill's trade had gotten into his body were less visible. Some festered for years before making themselves known.

One story I tell about why I ended up with university degrees is that, while an eighteen-year-old working at Birds Eye, I saw a woman get her twenty-year pin for working there. That sent me running back to college.

Three adult children of an alcoholic. More than once, when trying to be clever, I have framed a major difference among us this way: I married a man unlike our father; Diana married men like our father; Bill became our father.

There's as much falsehood in that as truth, nor does it explain much of anything. It doesn't explain why I still cared enough about Bill to be eating breakfast with him. Nor does it explain why he cared enough about our having rolled newspapers together when we were kids to suggest meeting at a diner across from where that had happened.

When the waitress came by with the coffee pot asking Bill and me if we wanted our cups topped off, I told her I'd take the check. Even as I left the tip, I knew it should have been more generous. Having been a waitress myself, once upon a time, I knew waiting tables was a tough gig.

I hugged Bill before getting back into my rental. As I drove toward my meeting with the grant officer, it occurred to me that I, not my brother, was the one who had escaped our family's gravitational field. I wonder whether Bill resented that as much as I had envied his freedom when we were children.

CHAPTER 6

Not Seeing the Whole Chessboard

By the time two years had passed since Bill's initial health crisis, Steve and I were spending every Sunday morning in the town of Spirit Lake, Idaho, an hour's drive from Spokane. Steve had taken on the role of interim minister of a small Presbyterian church there. He and I would always arrive in Spirit Lake early enough that he would have an hour and a half before Sunday worship started to get ready. While Steve prepared for the service, I would spend an hour walking the town's mainly deserted streets and roads.

Spirit Lake had one grocery store—unless you counted the two gas station mini-marts. There were as many biker bars as churches, and more moldering single-wide trailers than lakeside estates. Walking only a few blocks in any direction brought me to dirt roads leading into the forest, where firs and birches climbed up the steep slopes of the town's namesake lake. I routinely used part of my walking time to check in with Bill.

The drive to Spirit Lake on country roads that snaked around the base of Mount Spokane often gave me something to tell Bill: a flock of wild turkeys Steve had had to brake for because they were too stupid to get off the road, a herd of elk grazing in a meadow, an eagle perched atop a tamarack behind a horse pasture. These all became something to talk about in addition to Bill's medical appointments and treatments.

Though marrying a man unlike my father doesn't explain everything about me, its significance cannot be dismissed. We met in high school when he was a senior and I a sophomore. When Steve went off to college, we kept in touch through weekly phone calls and more frequent letters, seeing each other in the summers. We each kept all those letters. The two boxes have gone with us unopened through all our moves, like reliquaries. Their aura emanates from their existence, not from their contents. Steve's youngest sister Sherry likes to kid him that he's lucky to have married a saint, implying that only a saint would put up with her brother. If sainthood has to do with unbegrudgingly sacrificing for the good of another, I'm the one who lucked into marrying one.

Most faculty openings in philosophy had hundreds of applicants. After finishing graduate school, I had to search nationally. For my first faculty position, as a short-term sabbatical replacement, I was able to commute from where we had lived for a decade. But we had to move ninety miles north of Seattle for my second temporary job. For that move, Steve left his work and became a househusband. He was the only man standing at the bus stop, waiting for our older son Paul to be picked up for kindergarten. The moms treated him as a mascot, inviting him to join them for the coffee group after the kids were on the bus.

When I was offered a tenure-track job at Hope College in Michigan, Steve agreed to move for the second time in two years, this time twenty-three hundred miles to a place he'd never seen. Steve's first year there was tough. There, a man who had no ready answer to the question "What do you do?" was unusual to say the least. At first, Steve's life had little structure beyond taking care of the boys and sending out job applications. We'd almost given up on his finding a church position when he was hired as an associate pastor at a large congregation five miles from where we lived. Steve took all those risks for me unbegrudgingly.

Marrying early resulted in Steve and I spending the first fifteen years of our marriage taking turns as the full-time student. After Steve and I stopped taking turns going to school, we took our turns being the supportive spouse. Steve did his share of being the faculty husband, then the dean's husband, then the provost's husband. He made conversation across tables at dinner events at Hope College, then at Whitworth University, most of the time looking interested even when he was not. I had donned my pastor's wife persona in Holland, Zeeland, Standale, and Forest Grove, Michigan, and then in Idaho and eastern Washington.

Meanwhile, Bill gave me ample opportunities to see that, in contrast to my husband, I'm a begrudger to my bones. For one thing, I resented Bill's seeming lack of interest in Steve. The life that my husband and I shared was something about which Bill seemed incurious.

Perhaps my longest-standing grudge, aside from Bill's freedom to go where he pleased when we were young children, concerned Bill's behavior at my in-laws' house. Steve finds my sentimentality about his parents' house amusing. To him, it was one of several houses that he had lived in growing up, and one he lived in for only two years before just spending summers there while going to Stanford. But for me, that house was the quintessential stable place, a place of uncomplicated celebration that Steve and I went back to no matter where we moved. "Going home" meant going there—my mother's and siblings' make-do lives making for only makeshift homegoing.

When Steve and I started dating, I was attracted by his intelligence, his kindness, his height and—let's face it—his house. The Simon living room, used only for company, always looked ready for a photo shoot. Even the family room furniture had a tasteful look. On special occasions, Steve's family used real silver, Lenox china, and crystal goblets. My family's only flatware came from the S&H Green Stamp store. Our special dishes—the ones that were not Melmac—came plate by plate, bowl by bowl, and cup and saucer by cup and saucer, from points earned by purchases at the grocery store. "He didn't mean to break them," my mother said more than once, remembering the time that, somehow, when Dad was in the kitchen, most of those grocery store dishes had come tumbling down.

Steve's father was an insurance agent whose relaxed charm made him a gracious host. He would pour himself and his wife drinks from an actual liquor cabinet. Often dry sherry for Steve's mom, Grace. Always a vodka and tonic, measured out with a shot glass, for him. Never more than two drinks on weeknights, perhaps three on a weekend. My father, when he was drinking, kept the scotch on the highest shelf in the kitchen cabinet, as if keeping it up there fooled mom, or us kids, or himself about how fast its contents disappeared.

Long before my mother's death, my in-laws' house had come to feel like my family homestead. After her death, it became, in a more attenuated way, Bill's homestead too. Bill ate many Thanksgiving and Christmas dinners there. He spent considerable time on their patio during summer visits when Steve and I brought our sons to Portland from Michigan. Steve's parents treated my brother as an honorary Simon. But when Bill was at my in-laws, my anxiety over his behavior spoiled my enjoyment because he often violated what I saw as Simon rituals.

Bill's pouring his own drinks rather than waiting for Virg's "Can I get you another?" made me cringe. Though we were adult children of an alcoholic, Bill and I both chose to drink. We differed in that my brother never counted his drinks, while I always counted mine—and his too, anxiously, especially when we were with Steve's family. I learned Simon-family ways through emulation. I could have taken Bill aside for catechesis, but I did not. I noticed Grace and Virg noticing these things, though as good hosts, they said nothing. The best picture I have of Bill and me together was taken at their house. We are seated, smiling directly into the camara. Bill has a highball glass in his hand. My hands are wringing what looks like a cocktail napkin.

Another grudge I held against Bill was that, over the two and a half decades we lived in Michigan, he was our only immediate family member who never once visited us. He was also the only one of Paul's and Matt's aunts and uncles who had never sent them a birthday card. If my sons noticed this, they did not comment. They thought of

Uncle Bill as the cool guy who rode a Harley and played pool better than anyone. They'd seen him clear a pool table in more than one bowling alley before anyone else had sunk a ball.

In the summer of 2007, Steve's father, mother, sisters, and brother all made two trips to Michigan—one in June and one in August—to attend our sons' weddings. Bill had gotten wedding invitations, of course, but did not come. I had contemplated talking with Steve about offering to pay Bill's airfare to come to the weddings but decided not to. Steve's brother, John, was a carpenter and making less than Bill. John was taking unpaid time off to come. It wouldn't occur to him not to pay his own way. If Bill had cared enough, he could have found the means. Besides, I had enough to do as the mother of the grooms without being preoccupied with counting Bill's drinks.

In the case of Steve's parents, the effort to come to the weddings had been heroic. As Steve conducted Paul's and Julie's August ceremony, I spent most of my time willing my father-in-law, who was sitting next to me, not to collapse. He died four months later.

Simone Weil tells us that "when two beings who are not friends are near each other there is no meeting, and when two friends are far apart there is no separation." The part of the quote about people being near one another without meeting makes me think of my brother and me. Out of sight, out of mind—that's what we were to one another for so many years. Later, we were more often near, yet our attempts at connection often missed their mark. "When two friends are far apart there is no separation" makes me think of my relationship with my husband, especially during all those years we were dating via the United States Postal Service.

But Simone Weil is not giving relationship advice. Her remarks about friendship provide an entrée to accounting for how there is room for evil if the Creator of all things is wholly good. "Before all things, God loves himself. This love, this friendship of God, is the Trinity." Out of love, God makes room for the existence of creation, but to do this, a wrenching separation must occur within the Trinity.

The universe comes into being through Christ's self-emptying, which is at the same time the creation, the incarnation, and the crucifixion. This is her interpretation of the Bible's enigmatic reference to the Lamb of God slain from the foundation of the world.

During his crucifixion Christ continued to love God even in the face of experiencing God's abandonment. This opens the possibility of affliction being transformed into ultimate good through participation in Christ's cross. For Weil, Christology rescues affliction from pointlessness, though it remains an enigma nonetheless.

My brother Bill has not always been uncaring. Steve and I have a chess set. Its black squares and pieces are made of onyx; its "white" squares and pieces are actually made of streaked gray stone. Bill bought it in Mexico and gave it to us as a Christmas present a few years after we were married. That was back when he had the Texaco station. Back when I'd occasionally call him to ask advice about an estimate we'd been given on repairing our car. Back when Bill went places.

Every time I unpacked that chess set in whatever new apartment, then condo, then house we'd moved to, I thought of Bill. Though it's one of my cherished things, I care little for chess. Steve's the chess player, not I. I know how the pieces move but am seldom able to "see the board," as chess players say. I care about the chess set because Bill cared enough to carry its substantial weight home for our sake. That was back when Bill was living the dream, back when Steve and I had almost nothing but each other.

After my walks in Spirit Lake, I'd change my shoes and stand chatting with the congregation's early arrivers while pretending to sip the undrinkable coffee. In Spirit Lake, the chats during coffee hour were surprisingly interesting. I especially appreciated the story one man told of nearly hitting a moose while riding a motorcycle. By laying his bike down and sliding under the creature's belly, he'd lived to tell about it. Bill loved that story.

CHAPTER 7

Dorothy Day Never Knew My Brother

Two and a half years after Bill's initial hospitalization, I began making notes for a future book. I was doing a lot of reading about end-stage renal disease. I learned about how Willem Kolff developed the first artificial kidney in the Nazi-occupied Netherlands in the 1930s and 1940s. About how the first fifteen people Kolff treated died, and how the sixteenth lived for twenty-six days. About the technical improvements and delicate calculations needed to make long-term dialysis viable. About the toll that the lifesaving treatment enacts on the body. About how the United States dialysis industry's dominance by two large-scale providers, Fresenius and DaVita, affects per-patient cost. About health-care delivery to the working poor. Maybe I would figure out something worth saying—something others could benefit from.

The working title of my book project—which was mainly a self-soothing fantasy at that point—was *Dorothy Day Never Knew My Brother.* I had read Dorothy Day's *The Long Loneliness* two decades earlier, when I'd considered using it in a course. Dorothy Day, a Communist who converted to Catholicism, spent most of her life working with the destitute. By the 1980s, the Roman Catholic Church had already begun to consider whether to declare her a saint. Dorothy, bless her heart, thought that followers of Christ have no right to discriminate between the deserving and undeserving poor. In theory,

I saw the truth of what she said; after all, Jesus had said that every encounter with "the least of these" is an encounter with the ruler of creation. But I was finding Dorothy's dictum hard to live by.

Grudgingness stalked my every attempt to be openhanded in helping Bill. In my fantasy conversations with Dorothy Day, here are the kinds of things I told her:

- When Bill was well enough, Steve and I arranged to treat him to a restaurant dinner when we visited Portland. He'd choose the place and we'd meet him there. We'd arrive at the appointed time, and he'd walk out of the restaurant's bar carrying a half-finished drink. He'd order another as the waitperson gave us our menus. And another halfway through the meal. Along with those, he'd drink two glasses of water. All told, it was more fluid ounces of liquid than a dialysis patient should have had all day.
- Though Bill was still only spottily compliant with the dietary and lifestyle advice he was getting, he thought he knew more than his health care providers. Perhaps at times, he did. But mostly he was looking for medical work-arounds to the self-discipline needed to cope with dialysis treatment—work-arounds that did not exist.
- Although he had reached the point in his recovery when moving more would benefit him, Bill pressured his landlord to designate the parking place closest to his apartment a handicapped spot. He got what he wanted, but also earned the ire of his apartment manager.
- Bill acquired a cat and claimed it was a therapy animal so he wouldn't have to pay a pet deposit. When the manager expressed incredulity, Bill got his doctor to write him a prescription for the cat. The manager's irritation escalated.
- Bill had gotten the cat for free from an ad on craigslist—an ornery black beauty with startling translucent green eyes. Bill named him "Little Willy." What does it say about someone when they name a pet after themselves?

- I asked Bill what he wanted for Christmas, hoping to get him something that would be of genuine use or give him real joy. He said he'd like a power recliner. I suggested that he find one he liked and let us know how much it cost. He picked out a recliner that cost twice as much as any chair Steve and I had ever owned. I wrote him a check but did not use that strategy with him again.

And what would Dorothy Day say back to me, this woman who said, "There are two things you should know about the poor. They tend to smell, and they are ungrateful"? It was not hard to guess. *Carol, your list—the very fact that you are keeping score—is a two-edged sword. Get the log out of your own eye, girl.* And what would I say back? I was still working that out.

Neither Steve nor I were thinking of retiring immediately, but we had reached the age when we knew we should start thinking about whether we'd ever be able to afford to. So, we made an appointment with a man we knew and liked who was a certified financial planner. The first thing he did was ask us about our estimated monthly financial needs, our health, and our family. *Are there any members of your family you might need to help financially? Children? Parents?*

Steve mentioned that his mother was in an assisted living facility and had health problems. He also said that he thought she had enough money of her own to pay for her needs, barring unforeseen circumstances.

I mentioned Bill's situation. I gave the financial consultant an estimate of how much we'd been giving Bill annually but said that that amount might go up. *Could there come a time when he'll need to live with you?* I said I didn't know. I also mentioned that we were lending him our car.

I'd advise you not to do that. If he's in an accident and at fault and causes serious personal injury to someone else, it's you that someone who wants to sue will come after, not him. Your pockets are deeper than his. He told us to either ask for the car back or give it to Bill. *It's cleaner if you sell it to him for a dollar.*

So, the next time we went to Portland, we took the title to the car along and did just that. It would not have surprised Dorothy Day one bit that Bill did not say thank you. Nor that when he sold his motorcycle, he added not one penny to the dollar he gave us in exchange for our Malibu.

The day he sold his Harley was a sad one indeed. He'd lost hope of regaining the strength needed to hold the bike up while getting the kickstand down so he could dismount. Steve and I had had to use trial and error to access Bill's accounts and handle his affairs while he was unconscious in the ICU. When he recovered, I asked Bill to create a list of passwords and anything else we should know. At the bottom of that one-page sheet with the accounts and codes, right above "Cremation okay," Bill had typed "My bucket list—a motorcycle trip to see the country at my leisure." He now knew he would never live that dream.

As Bill's neediness pressed harder against my life, I began wishing I'd never heard of Dorothy Day. Oddly, that wish only intensified after Bill stopped drinking.

Bill's life had reached a modicum of equipoise, a fragile, quirky stability. He had become fluent in the language of creatinine, urea nitrogen, and albumin levels. He knew how tricky it was to calculate what his "dry weight" should be on any given day. Often when I asked, "How is it going?" he'd tell me about the excruciating cramps from dialysis and the exhaustion afterwards. But many times, he'd say, "Things have been pretty good." One time he told me about a fellow patient who he'd been giving rides to and from the dialysis center because the man's wife was too sick to drive him.

Months of suffering the side effects of dialysis had strengthened Bill's already strong desire to get on the kidney transplant list. One requirement of getting onto the list was having someone who is willing to companion you through the whole of the process—going to all the prequalification and postqualification appointments. I gathered that the point of this is twofold: It demonstrates that the potential organ recipient has the requisite social support network for success, and it ensures good communication by providing the same second set of ears listening at each step of the complicated journey. Astonishingly, a man named Joe, a recently acquired friend of Bill's, had stepped up to be this for Bill. I was intrigued by the fact that he told Bill he was doing this because he was a Christian.

But Bill ran into another, higher hurdle. Untreated alcoholics don't get put on the list. Bill's doctors would not give up their suspicion that he was one. That made him furious, but arguing with them was getting him nowhere. Denial is, after all, a symptom of alcoholism.

Bill knew that the only way to show that he was not an alcoholic was to quit drinking. But going to a treatment center would be admitting that his doctors were right. Instead, he set up his own support system. He stopped keeping alcohol in his apartment. He also enlisted the help of the bartender at Chan's. She agreed to serve him nothing but water or soft drinks, even if he asked for something else.

I'd watched my dad detox on his own once or twice. He'd lie on the family room floor, sweating and groaning. He'd twitch. He'd drink a lot of water. When he felt better, he'd make batches of homemade fudge. The Miller men were stubborn, tough. Sometimes that served them well. Often it did not.

Shortly after Bill stopped drinking, he became hyperaltruistic. First, he allowed a neighbor he hardly knew to sleep at his place because the man's apartment needed to be treated for toxic mold. Bill got irritated with the guy when he complained about Little Willy getting into his stuff. They were both relieved when the man went back to his own place. Then Bill bought a gas grill he could not afford and posted fliers around his building inviting people to build community by coming to a cookout. After that, he started talking about starting a new religion that sounded suspiciously like the plot of the old movie *Pay It Forward*.

I didn't know what to make of it. Was he hoping that someone he provided with a free burger would volunteer to give him a kidney? Was he hedging his bets in case there really was some final judgment?

Soon after that, Bill called just before midnight from an after-hours pet emergency clinic. He needed my credit card number, without which they would not touch Little Willy. Bill was sure that Willy would die without immediate care. The cat was a dependent living being that Bill loved. How could I say no? Steve and I ended up paying a vet bill for over $2,000 dollars. Had Willy swallowed some stray medications of Bill's? Contracted some real disease? I have no idea, because soon after that Bill began careening between emergency rooms, once or twice weekly, for a month.

One night he called and talked nonstop for twenty minutes. Every fourth or fifth word was "symptoms." When I finally was able to piece together that he was calling from a hospital, I had Steve use his cell phone to call the emergency room of the one nearest Bill's apartment. He used his ministerial status: Rev. Simon calling to find out about William Miller. He was told that, yes, Mr. Miller was there. He was in an exam room, but they were finding it impossible to treat him because he wouldn't get off the phone.

When I persuaded Bill to hand his phone to the doctor, the doctor asked if Bill had ever had a psychotic break and whether it was likely that he was taking drugs. I said no. I said that he had recently stopped drinking. *Could this be alcohol withdrawal?* The doctor neither endorsed nor denied that hypothesis but asked for my permission to give Bill a sedative. After concluding that he was experiencing symptoms of hypoxia from his failing heart, they got him stabilized and discharged him without admitting him to the hospital.

A week later, I got a call from Bill from the waiting room of an emergency room on the opposite side of Portland. He had been at a restaurant with a friend and passed out. He'd regained consciousness quickly, but the friend had driven him to the ER. The ER admissions staff were keeping him in the waiting room. He wanted me to call them and tell them that he needed to be admitted as soon as possible. He was sure that otherwise he was going to die.

That hospital did eventually admit him. I called to check on him each day, and on day two they said that he was under restraint because he'd been lashing out at the nurses and other attendants.

They'd had to call security. On day three, I was able to talk to him. "What happened?" he asked. Too large a question to be answered with the fragments of facts at my disposal.

This time they concluded that Bill's problem was caused by a drug interaction between one of his prescription meds and an over-the-counter antihistamine he was taking for hay fever. They told him to stop the antihistamine. The psychotic symptoms stopped.

During this stretch of our lives, I called Bill daily, certain that on any given day I would call and get no answer, and then a welfare check would find him dead.

To this day, I wonder about Bill's conviction that night in the after-hours pet clinic that Willy was desperately ill. Was that all part of Bill's downward psychological spiral? I'll never know. What I do know is that Little Willy lived on. So did Bill, for more years than I could have guessed at the time.

After that chaotic period, Bill's life took an upward turn. He survived a heart valve replacement and the repair of another valve. Once he recovered from that operation, he had more energy. He succeeded in getting into the Section 8 housing program and moved into a building only a few blocks from his old apartment. It was down the block from Chan's and, unlike his old place, it had interior hallways and keypad locks on the exterior doors. The view from his third-floor apartment was a landscaped area that lifted my spirits each time I saw it. A slider gave access to a small balcony with room for two chairs.

His friends Robin, Rachel, and Pete moved Bill's things for him. His former landlord was, no doubt, relieved to see him go. As a housewarming gift, we got Bill a loveseat that fit the compact living room it shared with his recliner, small desk, curio cabinet, and the platform for his large TV.

When I visited Bill, I emptied the neglected litter box, cleared the kitchen counters, stocked the refrigerator, and cooked and froze meals. At his insistence, I also bought the ten-for-ten-dollar, sodium-loaded frozen entrees he liked—a poor choice for someone on dialysis.

During most of the time that I was in his apartment, Bill would sit in his recliner and watch sports on his huge flat-screen TV, with the sound muted or low so that we could talk. By the time I first saw Bill's new apartment, one side of the loveseat already showed snags from Little Willy's claws. From visit to visit, I monitored, without comment, the progression of the damage.

I never did use Dorothy Day's *The Long Loneliness* in a course, even though I taught one called "Saints, Heroes, and Ordinary People." The course arose from my long-standing interest in the topic of supererogation—a big word for performing actions that go beyond what's morally required. Most people are helpful to a decent degree and refrain from wanton harm. Many consider anything they do beyond that as a kind of moral extra credit. There are puzzles here. Where is the line between minimal decency and heroism or saintliness? How much potential risk or inconvenience gets us off the moral hook?

Christian doctrine raises an additional puzzle. Can any action, no matter how costly, count as supererogatory, given what I owe in gratitude to a God who has made the infinite sacrifice of suffering and dying on my behalf? Yet even Protestants will see a Dorothy Day or a Mother Teresa as extraordinary, though they may not see them as saints in any fuller sense than any other Christian is.

I decided that Day's life was too extraordinary to fit my "Saints, Heroes, and Ordinary People" course's theme. I hoped the three concepts in the course's title would be lenses through which students could envision the lives they hoped to lead. That entailed helping them to see that being ordinary didn't give them an excuse for living a slacker life.

The saintly Catholic I used instead of Day was Thérèse of Lisieux. She had authored *The Story of a Soul* when she was around the same age as my students. Though her life was markedly different from theirs, she thought of herself as ordinary. She called herself Jesus's little flower. How could you not love a twenty-three-year-old who says things like, "The sun shines equally both on cedars and on every tiny flower. In just the same way God looks after each soul as if it had no equal"?

To appeal to male students who took my course, I almost always included a book about military heroism. Often that book was *Flight to Arras*, a memoir in which Antione de Saint-Exupéry is trying to figure out whether what he is doing is pointless. He's a reconnaissance pilot whose mission might be fatal and is certain to be futile. France's retreating army has no way of using the information he's gathering by flying over enemy territory. The book has the advantage of being short. And it has drama. Life or death situations. But *Flight to Arras* is really an extended rumination taking place in the cockpit of a plane. I have long loved the book, not for its plot or premise, but for its prose.

I included saintly Protestants by having students read Philip Hallie's *Lest Innocent Blood Be Shed: The Story of the Village of Le Chambon and How Goodness Happened There*. Hallie describes how a church's network of Bible study groups turned into a resistance movement that sheltered Jews during the Nazi occupation of southern France. Hallie found a striking conviction among the villagers in Le Chambon. Most of them thought that putting their own lives at risk to save strangers was what any decent person would do. Le Chambon lies on a plateau in southern France, and Hallie uses that as a metaphor for understanding their attitude. When you live on a plateau, you do not notice your altitude. If courage and altruism come naturally to you, you cannot imagine acting differently.

I paired Hallie's book with a segment from the show *60 Minutes* in which a German Jewish man, who as a boy was hidden under floorboards in the home of Protestant neighbors, is interviewed along with the daughter of the people who gave him shelter. The daughter recounted knowing that if her family were caught hiding Jews, she and her brother would have been hung from their balcony—she had seen this happen to others. There's a cost—often a supreme one—to being heroic and saintly. Toward the end of the interview, the man admitted that he could not have done what the people who saved him did. Perhaps he could have put himself at risk, but he could not have risked his children. The people who hid him were saints; he was not.

Could I respond to Dorothy Day's *Get the log out of your own eye, girl* by saying, *Lady, you were a saint; I am not*? Only if I wanted to hear her ask, *So, you're saying that as far as you're concerned, the gospel is moot?* I pictured her shaking her head in disgust. Not at Bill. At me. As self-soothing fantasies, my conversations with Dorothy were not going well.

During the roughest times with Bill, I thought that my imaginings of Dorothy Day, St. Thérèse, Philip Hallie, and Antoine de Saint-Exupéry were ganging up on me. In *Flight to Arras*, Saint-Exupéry keeps harping on countries and farms being webs woven by the sum of their gifts—each gift strengthening the whole while fulfilling the giver. He might as well have added "families" to countries and farms, and put it in big, bold type. His phrases that pierced me most were "Fraternity is the creation of sacrifices alone," and "To create love, we must begin by sacrifice." But how much sacrifice?

Simone Weil claims that, because affliction transforms a person into something repulsive ("a half-crushed worm writhing on the ground"), compassion for the afflicted is a miracle, like walking on water. Only pure saints can pull it off. Yet Christianity elevates ordinary people, claiming that every person has inestimable potential. In the Greek and Roman world, heroes were a category unto themselves. No ordinary person could be expected to act like Achilles or Antigone or Aeneas. But Christianity calls us to be perfect as God is perfect, even while confessing our shortcomings and dependence on grace. At least in that way, life was simpler for Greeks and Romans than it is for those of us for whom being ordinary doesn't get us off the moral hook. Most non-Christians admire a Dorothy Day or a Mother Teresa, but few see their example as calling their own lives into question as, arguably, Christians should.

Sure, brother dear, take my car, my credit card number, my money, and my time. But can I draw the line at my kidney?

CHAPTER 8

Stung

As Bill and I talked more frequently than we ever had, I learned that we had more in common than I had known. I found out that, as siblings raised by a mother who never missed an episode of *Perry Mason*, we both self-soothed with reruns of *Law & Order*. More significantly, as Bill recounted stories of his latest conversation with a doctor, nurse, or technician, I realized that we shared a sharp tongue and an impatience with fools. We both made hasty judgments about others' foolishness.

With one another, we were more diffident. Though I thought *Bill, you fool!* a thousand times, I didn't ever blurt, "You've got to be kidding me" or say, "You know, you really shouldn't eat that (drink that, do that)." But perhaps I didn't need to. Perhaps he read me the way I could read him—knowing his unspoken frustration, from the way his voice caught in his throat when he was clenching his jaw as we talked on the phone.

One time, for whatever reason, I told him about my dream of us as small children in a driverless car rolling down a hill. Bill said, "I have something like that." He went on to tell me about his own bad downhill-car-ride dream. He is descending Mount Hood as his brakes fail. For a while, he successfully struggles to keep the car on the road, but he ends up crashing.

Another time, I was with him when we were getting onto a down escalator. He was just ahead of me. I saw him do an involuntary stutter step. "Hey," I said, "I do that too." Neither of us knew why.

Bill and I also found that our memories sometimes diverged. What I remembered most about our father's death was how, as a twenty-one-year-old junior at the University of Oregon, I'd been unequipped to mourn. When Mom called the day that Dad died, I answered, but she asked to talk to Steve. Mom could not bear to tell me directly that Dad was dead. I sat next to Steve in numb silence as he drove us from Eugene to Portland. By the time we got to my parents' house, Mom's minister was there, along with my brother and sister. They were sitting at the dining room table discussing the funeral.

My mother recounted again how Dad had died. He'd been raking leaves on that cold November day. A neighbor boy saw him fall to the ground. The child ran home to get his father, who was a fireman. When the man let himself in through the back gate, he found my father unresponsive. He tried CPR, but Wesley Miller's life was gone. The EMT attendants said it was a heart attack.

What Bill remembered most about the funeral was his anger at Wes Jr., our half-brother. I barely remembered Wes Jr.'s having been there. I know nothing about Dad's first marriage beyond its having produced a son. Our half brother was old enough to have been in an army uniform in my first memory of him. I saw him from time to time while growing up, but I thought of him as more like a distant uncle than a brother. I had not realized that Bill had looked up to him as a hero.

I could hear the disgust in my brother's voice as he told me how, after Dad died, he desperately wanted Wes Jr.'s affirmation of his ability to step into what he saw as his new role as man of the Miller house. He wanted Wes Jr.'s assurance that he was up to being the strong one for the sake of his grieving mother and younger sisters. Instead, Wes Jr. used the opportunity to try to put the fear of God into Bill. He told Bill he'd better get right with his Maker.

I recognized Wes Jr. instantly in this story. He became a Christian in his thirties or forties, something he credited to my mother's influence. He had seemed rigid even to my past rigid self. Yet I did find Bill's story surprising. It had never occurred to me that Bill would see himself as the man of the Miller house. Now that he said it, it had such an of-course-ness about it that I realized how self-absorbed I'd been at the time. Stupefied by my own grief, I don't think I gave a moment's thought to how Bill or Diana was doing.

What I remembered was that Mom had gone along with my idea to keep Dad's casket closed. At that point, the only funeral I had attended was for a high school friend who had died, along with her baby, in some catastrophe of teenage childbirth. When our grandparents, whom we kids barely knew, died, our parents had held their grief over those deaths tight and hidden. Death skulked in my imagination as fearsome and shameful, though as a Christian I was supposed to believe that death was gain—a going home to the Lord. "That body is not Dad," I had insisted.

I remember asking the minister to read John Donne's "Death Be Not Proud" at the service. I knew much later that that was a mistake. Neither my father nor most others at the funeral cared about poetry. Even those who believed, with Donne, that death would ultimately die knew that death's sting is real. Death stung so much that I could not look at my father dead.

An eldest son born in 1950s America sees himself as the successor, upon his father's death, to household headship. How could that surprise the younger sister, raised as they both were? And how would that sister's proneness to surprise, if he sensed it, make the brother feel?

Oddly, in retrospect, writer Karen Olsson's book about Simone Weil's relationship with her own brother, André, helped me understand what puzzled me about the dynamic between Bill and me while he was alive. The oddity lies in the stark differences between Simone and André's upbringing and Bill's and mine. The Weil siblings' father was a wealthy Parisian doctor; their mother was a homeschooler par excellence. Long before their teenage years, Simone and André had become fluent enough in ancient Greek to use it as a secret oral language between them.

Neither Bill nor I had either the innate brilliance or the privileged upbringing of André and Simone. But what we did share was birth order and early closeness, the dynamic of a first-born male child and his adoring younger sister. And like the Weil siblings, Bill and I shared the firm belief that the older brother was smarter than the younger sister. Learning came easily to Bill, while my dyslexia made learning a slog.

Karen Olsson describes Simone and André as "yin-yang children who shaped and were shaped by each other." She describes André as expansively self-assured while Simone felt herself too young and too different from him to ever catch up. Bill was bold while I was shy, athletic while I was clumsy. He was yang. I was yin.

Karen Olsson, like several other commentators, interprets many of Simone Weil's actions as a quest for self-punishment. Weil not only sought out hard labor but wanted to be parachuted behind enemy lines during WWII so that she could care for the wounded (her family, given their Jewish roots, had fled France by this time). When she was unsuccessful in convincing anyone to help her with this plan, she went to work for the French Resistance operating from London. While living in London, she refused to eat more than what she imagined prisoners and peasant children in occupied France were allowed.

Olsson is not the first to speculate that Weil's appetite for suffering was rooted in her sense that, unlike her brother, she would never measure up. Well before Simone died at thirty-four, André had become a theoretical mathematician of international repute, while the publications that would earn her international acclaim would come out posthumously. The cause of Simone's death was tuberculosis made worse by her refusal to eat. The debate over her identification with those who were suffering continues. Some see it as a function of her fierce determination to align her life with her ideals regarding love. Others see it as rooted in a clinical disorder.

What if André's yang and Simone's yin had begun to reverse in their mid-twenties? How would André have reacted if, instead of a continued upward trajectory, he had experienced significant professional disappointment in his mid-twenties? Would he have become bitter in midlife and resentful toward his younger sister, especially if she surpassed his and her own expectations for intellectual achievement?

Bill's aspirations were nothing like André's. Like many males from lower-middle-class households, he wanted upward mobility, increasing success, continued control. My aspirations were different than my brother's. (Well, maybe not altogether different; what was my infatuation with my in-laws' house about, if not a desire for upward mobility?) What I wanted most was to satisfy my intellectual curiosity, make unlikely connections, and get to the bottom of things. Life nonetheless gave me upward mobility and a modicum of success, while the longer Bill lived, the less of those he experienced. It never occurred to me to see Bill and me in competition with one another, but looking back I can see how my becoming more yang while he became more yin must have stung. Could that be at least part of why he never came to visit us in Michigan? Was another part of it finding my husband's ministerial profession off-putting, given the bruises left by Wes Jr.'s floundering attempts at evangelism?

Our mother's grief after her husband's death was palpable, though she did not cry in front of us. As we gathered at her house that first Christmas Eve, only a few weeks after his death, we saw she had gone and bought gifts, wrapping them for all of us and asking Steve to pass them out as Dad would have done. She'd taped tags with the names of the recipients on them but left a blank after "From." She was not ready yet to write "Mom" without "and Dad."

Dad had not made a will, which created complications for Mom. Their joint bank account was frozen for a while. He had worked for the same company for almost forty years, but he had not designated beneficiaries. So, Dad's pension was divided between his wife and children: My mother got half; the other half was split among his children. I do not know what my mother's portion was, but it could not have been much. For over forty-five years I have gotten $57 once a month from my father's pension. Unlike Willy Loman, Dad's mortgage was not paid off. Unlike Loman's wife, Linda, my mother could not say, "We're free and clear."

But my father was not improvident. He had a small life insurance policy that helped replace his salary for a time. He also left behind cases of canned goods, which he had routinely bought whenever they were on sale. He'd done the grocery shopping. Mom, who handled the family finances, gave Dad a grocery budget. He made a game of seeing how much he could underspend his grocery allowance, going to multiple grocery stores each week to take advantage of sales. He banked whatever excess he didn't spend on scotch. When he'd accumulated enough, he'd pay cash for a new car. My mother took years to use up all the cans of tomato sauce, corn, peas, and green beans.

Living with Wes had not been easy; living without him would be no easier. Mom sold their house less than a year after he died, using the equity to buy a double-wide trailer. Unlike the mortgage payment, the monthly fee for the lot in the mobile home park was affordable on her bookkeeper's salary.

In the immediate aftermath of our father's death, Bill, Diana, and I each reacted differently. Within a year, Diana got married to a man named Richard, whom she had met at work. Richard seemed pleasant enough, but because Steve and I were living elsewhere, I barely got to know him. The marriage did not last long. Like our father, Richard had a drinking problem. Unlike our father, he was a violent drunk. Diana ended their marriage after Richard put a dent in their drywall with his fist during one of their arguments.

Around that same time, just as I was finishing my undergraduate degree, I caused a marital crisis. Looking back, I associate that troubled time metaphorically with a canoe trip Steve and I took when dating. We were on the Russian River in northern California. The river's depth kept changing, and stretches were so shallow that we had to pick up the canoe and carry it until we reached a place where it would not scrape the gravelly riverbed. Other stretches were deep, with rushing water and strong currents. On one swift bend in the river, the current was carrying our canoe toward large metal structures along the bank that looked like giant toy jacks made of rebar. Though we were paddling hard, our canoe kept getting closer to the spikes sticking out over the water at chest height. Panicking, I jumped, overturning the canoe and dumping Steve into the river. The current's force held our submerged canoe firmly up against the bank—wedged against the giant jacks that, I suppose, were erosion-prevention structures. Prying the canoe loose was a struggle, with Steve doing most of the work. After emptying the canoe of water, we got back in. I was shaken, mortified, grateful. All Steve said was, "Could you please just try to stay in the canoe?"

Our early marital pain had no more to do with fleeing Steve than my jumping from that canoe. My amateur psychological diagnosis is that the looming blankness of a post-graduation future and suppressed grief over my father's death spooked me into short-lived wanderlust. A few times in my life, wisdom has come to me like a jolt of Narcan. This was one of those times. But repairing our marriage was arduous and full healing took its own sweet time.

Bill's fortunes, on the other hand, seemed at that point to be looking up. Not long after our father died, Mom lent Bill money to buy his Texaco gas station dealership. I suppose it must have been money left over from the sale of her house. He built a client base that valued his skill as a mechanic and his business soon became a thriving concern. He reinvested some of his profits back into buying more sophisticated equipment for the car repair side of his business.

Bill also took an active role in Oregon's statewide gas station dealers association, testifying before the state legislature in a successful attempt to keep customers from being able to pump their own gas. The dealers lobbied for the restriction as a safety issue, but in truth they were trying to stem the tide against the demise of gas stations as full-service providers of auto care. Dealers did not want to become owners of mini-marts with adjacent pumps.

Bill did not live to see Oregon's ban on pumping your own gas lifted, but long before he died, Oregon gas stations followed the nationwide trend of replacing repair bays with mini-marts. That's what happened to the station he had owned as soon as his franchise reverted to Texaco. That was salt in Bill's wound over his bankruptcy. How much more must it have stung to go from being the man of the Miller house to being the defaulter on the loan he'd gotten from his mother?

Simone Weil tells us that the threshold between affliction and other kinds of suffering is affected by an array of personal factors. The event or set of circumstances may plunge one person into affliction but not another. This may tempt us to think that affliction results from weakness—an inability to cope. Couldn't we all be the survivor who, after breaking his leg in the wilderness, makes a splint from tree limbs and limps out on his own?

Well, no. For Weil also tells us that affliction injects inertia into the soul, making the afflicted person complicit in his own affliction. Out of despair or a sense of unworthiness, those who are afflicted may even shun or flee the means of deliverance. "It is as though affliction had established itself in him like a parasite and were directing him to suit its own purposes," says Weil. I have often wondered how much of Bill's noncompliance with his dialysis regime was a symptom of affliction—an affliction that someone less in need of adventure and competition would not have experienced.

CHAPTER 9

Head of the House

In another conversation that Bill and I had, we found that our memories of our sister's death coincided up to a point, then veered off in differing directions.

A year after our sister Diana died, I had written a brief autobiographical piece entitled "Contending with Gentle Death." The title came from the essay's opening scene, where I'm processing in with the other faculty to Hope College's baccalaureate service on graduation day. In a few hours, I would fly out to be with Diana. Those in the chapel sang the processional hymn "All Creatures of Our God and King." Its lyrics are based on a prayer by St. Francis of Assisi. When we got to the final verse, I was too angry to sing. That last verse begins, "Oh, thou most kind and gentle death, waiting to hush our latest breath." I saw nothing kind about a brutal, fatal illness befalling someone I loved who was still days away from turning forty.

But at the end of that essay, I acknowledged that Diana, just after she died, had looked as if she'd been embraced by something kind and gentle. I thought she looked beatific. I'd even done a charcoal sketch of my memory of her, her head tilted, her eyelids half closed in hooded repose. The drawing accompanied the article when it appeared. I sent a copy to Bill shortly after it was published.

During one of our conversations, I mentioned that memory of Diana's deathbed and having written about it. Bill retorted, "Yah, I remember that article. I didn't tell you at the time, but I thought it was bullshit. I thought she looked dead."

For me, our sister's dying started the night in November 1994, when the phone rang just as I had fallen asleep. My mother and Diana were both on the other end of the line, which seemed ominous. It turned out that Mom was there as emotional support for both of her daughters. Diana said she didn't want me to worry, but she had breast cancer. She'd need a mastectomy, but they'd be doing radiation before surgery, so she wasn't sure about the timetable. Her tone was upbeat, rehearsed. I waited to cry until we hung up.

Among my first thoughts after hanging up the phone was: Oh my God, Michael will leave. He will leave her both sick and heartbroken. I had yet to meet Michael, the guy she was living with, whom she'd met in a karaoke bar. She'd shown me pictures. Handsome. Great hair. In his late thirties, but boyish looking. Before moving in with Diana, he'd been living with his mother. His two-year-old son lived with the child's mother.

Michael didn't leave Diana. Instead, he proposed to her the day after she had a double mastectomy. Their wedding was five months later, after she was done with her rounds of chemo and her hair had grown back, in the clubhouse of the housing development where Michael's mother lived. Steve officiated the ceremony. I was Diana's matron of honor. Her nephews, my sons, were Michael's groomsmen, which was touching, but made me wonder whether Michael had any close friends.

Six months after the wedding, Diana's cancer recurred. Resuming chemotherapy did little to slow the cancer's spread through multiple organs and into her bones. She sounded more frightened each time I called her. The day after the academic year ended, I flew from Michigan to Portland to help.

When I arrived, I found a mess. The double-wide trailer—the same one Mom had lived in until she'd moved into a seniors-only apartment house—was full of Michael's possessions layered helter-skelter with Diana's. There was hardly room to move. Diana loved to create order. Squalor was not natural to her. Like her cancer, it was an invader. Diana was much too sick to have done any cleaning for weeks, maybe months. Michael, who was meticulous about the cleanliness of his clothes and body, did no housework beyond laundry. The kitchen floor was crusted with dirt. One corner held a stack of empty pizza boxes. The carpet was covered with cat hair. Mom, who lived nearby, had repeatedly asked whether she could come over. Diana put her off, wanting to hide the disarray. Now she was too sick to care.

Powerless to address the cancer, I set to work on the squalor. I scrubbed the kitchen floor on my knees while Diana slept. I rented a storage unit, moving enough into it to make space in the living room for the hospital bed that hospice delivered. As I sorted through unpaid bills, I saw that Michael had run the two of them into suffocating debt.

Michael spent most of the time I was there out of the house, ostensibly working. I began to suspect that he had proposed to Diana so he could inherit the little she had. I viewed him as an invader in my sister's life, as, perhaps, he viewed me in his marriage. Who was I, he might have asked, to barge in, cleaning and sorting? Our antipathy remained masked by politeness. After all, what could be done now about my doubts? To this day, I am torn between regret for not saying, "Don't do it!" back when she'd first told me Michael was moving in and gratitude that she'd died married to a man whom I'd witnessed make her feel loved just by cupping her foot in his hand and saying her name. I hope—I need to believe—that is what she felt.

Our mother and Diana's friends, as well as her boss, were able to visit Diana during the last few days of her life in a setting that did not shame her. Though enjoyment was beyond any of us, Diana played her part as we gathered around her bed with balloons and gifts on her fortieth birthday.

The day after the party, Diana woke from a nap pleading, "I've been good. I've been good," like a child being led into a gas chamber.

All I could do was hold her hand and repeat, "Yes, yes, you have," feeling horrible that she might doubt my esteem, unsure she knew who I was, wondering if all my organizing had felt like blame.

For the next four days, Bill and I spent most of our time by her bedside. Michael was in and out.

All three of us were with her in her final hours, along with a competent, kind hospice nurse. The strong diaphragm developed by Diana's singing kept her breathing longer than any of us anticipated. At one point, Bill started repeating, "You're working too hard, Diana. Just let go." Michael said to no one in particular, "It's like she's in labor." Her gasps went on and on. After her breathing stopped, I thought she looked beatific, the hooded rest of her eyelids like that of saints in icons.

Within an hour after Diana died, Bill had driven me over to Mom's so that we could break the news together. Though she must have known why we were there when she buzzed us into the building's front entrance, she stiffened like she'd been slapped when we told her. Bill stayed only a few minutes, then went back, so Michael would not have to go through the removal of Diana's body on his own. I stayed until morning, so Mom would not be alone. Both Bill and I remembered all of that.

What I could not remember was what Bill had gone through when he went back to that double-wide trailer, what he only told me in that conversation three years before he died. "I thought she looked dead. There was nothing pretty that I saw. You weren't there when the undertakers came to take her. You didn't see how they had to tilt that damn gurney to get it out of the trailer's stinking door." I could hear in his frigid tone the pain he was reliving.

If I had been there, as Bill had, could I still have remembered seeing Diana as peaceful moments after her death? I'll never know.

I do know that Diana's death was a loss like no other for our mother. On our last family trip to Portland before Mom's death, Steve and I took her and our sons up to Mount St. Helens, the volcanic peak visible from Portland that had lost thirteen hundred feet of height in a cataclysmic eruption in 1980. I think Mom identified with that scarred mountain. The night of Diana's death, she told me that God only partially understood her pain, because God had experienced the death of a Son, not a daughter. I saw no sign that she held this shortcoming against God.

For three years after Diana's death, our mother ping-ponged from the hospital to an intermediate-care facility, and then back to her apartment, only to be readmitted to the hospital after a short time. The cause of each hospitalization was different—stubborn cellulitis in a leg, diverticulitis, a fall in a grocery store parking lot that signaled heart failure. Bill was the one who handled the bulk of all that endless worry and the work of Mom's transitions, as I was two thousand miles away in Michigan. I would swoop in periodically for a week at a time.

I remember making conversation with my mother's newish Baptist pastor in her hospital room one time during those months. The man asked me how I'd ended up teaching philosophy. I told him about growing up hearing my mother analyze, and often rebut, the Sunday sermon over pot roast each week. She did not doubt the minister's competence; rather she thought he'd done his job, and now she was doing hers. Her job was to examine whether he had good evidence for what he'd said and whether he had ignored a crucial point or scripture passage that, if he'd really cared about preaching the truth, would have been in that sermon somewhere. Mom's pastor responded, "I don't think you should blame her for this." He was quite serious.

But my mother was a better Baptist than her minister. She knew that practicing the priesthood of all believers requires discernment, which requires questioning. Christians I knew while growing up emphasized the importance of "strong faith." To many of them, strong faith meant unexamined belief. As a teenager with a questioning mind, I found that my mother's willingness to question lessened my discomfort with asking philosophical questions. Without her example, I doubt I could have become a philosopher without jettisoning my Christian faith.

Simone Weil asks us to consider the possibility—in fact, the actuality—that shipwrecks contribute to the beauty of the sea. The majesty of the sea is a function of its obedience to the laws of gravity and fluid dynamics. A sea that could change its ways at will to safely deliver all ships to their destinations would have ceased to be the sea and become a cartoon character (my analogy, not hers). Weil goes on to say something even more startling: "All the horrors which occur in this world are like the folds imposed upon the waves by gravity. That is why they contain an element of beauty."

In his poem, "The Wreck of the Deutschland," Gerard Manley Hopkins memorializes five nuns who died in a shipwreck along with two hundred others. The tallest of the nuns was heard repeatedly calling, "O Christ, Christ, come quickly." Hopkins imagines her seeing Christ in the storm—not as an apparition or vision, but *as* the storm. In calling Christ, the nun was christening "her wild-worst Best." Her single-sighted faith gives her the ability to see what remains hidden to others. Hopkins's poem inscribes the hope that the faith of the tall nun becomes an instrument of Providence, allowing those others who might have perished unrepentant to turn to God before they die.

I do not know whether Simone Weil ever read this poem, but if she had, I think she would have embraced Hopkins as a spiritual kinsman.

Diana's death raised the question, in differing ways for Bill and Mom and me, of how horror and beauty are related. I made my own attempt to make some beauty of it. I asked Michael for only a few of her things. One was a jade-green dress made of fabric that looked like silk brocade from her closet. Diana had looked splendid in that dress. Its vividness suited her. I wore it once, but it was loose on me in the wrong places. I cut it up and used it in a crazy quilt—a traditional memento mori. Along with the jade material, I used baby blue scraps from the dress I'd worn for Diana's wedding, along with black velvet, cobalt poplin, and bright multicolored fabric from a skirt she'd once given me. I embellished the quilt with several beadwork musical notes to honor Diana's love of music. Meager consolation for having her voice silenced so early.

I can project myself into Weil's and Hopkins's shared perspective, and even be awed by it, but it's not where I live and breathe. I believe, with Julian of Norwich, that God *will* make all things well. Does that mean that all the horrors of life *presently* contain elements of beauty? Not that I can see.

During the last years of Mom's life, Bill fulfilled his role as "head of the house." He took care of wrapping up her affairs after her death, which I pictured as simple enough, since by then Mom had given away almost everything she ever had. Though she'd experienced deep sadnesses, she had seen herself as blessed—blessed to be blessing, as she would often say—which was an identity she retained to her dying day. Mom had bought a double plot under a cedar tree when Dad died and ordered a double headstone in anticipation of her own death. Both their names had been engraved before it was installed. Bill took care of having her death date added. Bill also followed her wish to have her remains cremated and interred in her husband's plot, so that the plot next to them could be a resting place for himself. She had signed the deed to that plot over to Bill before her death.

I wondered only after Mom's death how much her toughness had been put on for my sake and Bill's. Was she taking care of us up to the end by minimizing how much more we—especially I—could have done to ease the hardships of her later years? Could I have seen through that ruse if I'd wanted to? Perhaps. If so, she would have forgiven me without my asking.

When I was sorting through Diana's unpaid bills during the week before she died, I found a thick manila envelope of yellowed legal correspondence among her things. These documents showed that our father had no birth certificate. In the late 1930s, he had hired a lawyer to try to find a doctor in the small Missouri town where he was born—the doctor who had handed his infant self to William and Carrie Miller. Hunting down that doctor allowed my father to prove he had been born in the United States.

Why did Diana have our father's papers? Why was I just finding out about them at forty-three? I did not ask. I did not ask Diana—or Mom—or Bill.

My not asking Diana makes sense to me. She was dying, after all. We were both focused on the enormity of that. Why did I not ask Mom? I could explain that away by guessing that I didn't want to bother her with questions as she sank into her final sadness. But why, over the course of our six years of conversations, did I never bring those documents up with Bill? The only sense that I can make of that is that I am a Miller.

Stutter-stepping at the top of escalators. Hanging back from asking. Thinking twice about—then never getting around to—telling. These are the things that Millers do.

CHAPTER 10

Stretching Out a Withered Limb

In 2017, almost three years into his life as a dialysis patient, Bill made it onto Oregon's kidney transplant list. He called to tell me the news on Ash Wednesday, a coincidence that meant nothing to him but had significance for me.

Bill's initial number was 261. Your number is only one of the factors considered in who gets the next available organ. If you and someone who is not as high on the list both match an available kidney, the other person might get it because she has a more pressing need for it at the time. There's a tricky balance: If you are too sick, you might be removed from the list because the surgery would be too risky; if you are not sick enough, you might have to wait longer. Given the imbalance between available organs and people who need them, many people on transplant lists die waiting. The way to escape the uncertainties of the list is to find your own donor kidney.

When Bill told me about the appointment when he'd gotten the news he said, "They wanted me to set up some Facebook plea for a live donor, but I said to hell with that. I don't see anyone stepping up to give me a kidney. That's okay. I can wait. Two years, maybe less, maybe more." I let that sit there between us without comment.

Some Christians give up something for Lent. Most years, I gave up alcohol as an annual check-in with myself about my life's center and circumference. One year I decided to give up grumbling.

I found I could go forty days without alcohol but caught myself grumbling within the first week. Calling it "debriefing," when I did it with a colleague, and "venting," when I did it with Steve as I told him about a frustrating meeting, didn't fool even me. Why, I wonder, is there no twelve-step program for grumblers? In 2017, my Lenten exercise was wrestling with whether to give Bill one of my kidneys.

How do you decide whether to become a live organ donor? If I were making an administrative decision, I would weigh the pros and cons. As I started doing research, I learned some things I had not known. For many years now, organ donation programs have used both direct and indirect donor matches. If Carol's kidney is a match for Bill, she can be his direct donor. But if Carol's kidney isn't a match for Bill, she can give her kidney to Sid and Sid's brother Ed, who is a match for Bill, can donate his kidney to Bill. Such happy coincidences are unlikely. Instead, there are complex chains that lead from the volunteer's kidney to a kidney that matches her loved one. I heard an interview on NPR with the computer scientist who developed the algorithm for these complex exchanges. You could hear pride and enthusiasm in his voice.

Another thing that surprised me is that the surgery is less complicated for the recipient than the donor. I had pictured Bill having a kidney removed and replaced with a new one—possibly mine. But his kidneys would be left where they are. The new kidney would be grafted in another location laparoscopically through a small incision. Removing the donated organ from the live donor is now often done laparoscopically as well, but some circumstances require a more invasive procedure.

The pros of live kidney donation are clear for recipients. Transplants using kidneys from live donors are more likely to be successful than kidney transplants from cadavers. And, other things being equal, successful transplant recipients live considerably longer, and suffer less, than dialysis patients. There are additional pros of having a relative who is willing to be your donor. Close relatives are more likely to be a match for you than any given random donor. Even if the relative is not a match, she can participate in an indirect match. Both direct and indirect donations substantially shorten the wait time for the person who needs a kidney. The longer a patient is on dialysis, the more likely it is that the transplant will fail when they do find a match.

But there are cons to consider, for both recipient and donor. Major surgery is always a risk, as informed consent documents remind you. I had to sign one when I had bunion surgery. The final risk on the list was "death." Postsurgical complications like infections are also a risk. Both the recipient and donor are certain to have substantial postsurgical pain. Most of the time this can be controlled with drugs, but not always. Even without complications, most recipients and donors will have a two- to four-month recuperation period before resuming work and normal activity levels.

The donor takes on the substantial risk of having no backup kidney if her remaining kidney fails. Nature builds in redundancy for a reason.

For the recipient, graft-versus-host disease is a risk. The recipient will be on antirejection drugs for the rest of his life. Those drugs have side effects, some of them serious, although many side effects can be managed with additional drugs.

Back when I was teaching Introduction to Symbolic Logic, I could have set this up as a story problem about kidney donation by a live donor. For any X who is a recipient and any Y who is a live organ donor:

- X gets to live longer than X would without the transplant.
- X can stop spending twelve hours a week undergoing dialysis. And X can escape dialysis's debilitating side effects sooner than if X waits for a random available organ match.
- X will need to be on antirejection drugs for the rest of X's life. Those drugs may cause side effects, ranging from acne, weight gain, and puffiness to more serious problems like bone thinning, diabetes, and being more susceptible to serious infection because his immune system is suppressed.

- If Y donates her kidney, Y's life is likely to go on as it would have after a few months of recovery, but there is some chance that Y will have shortened her life.

QED: Likely substantial gain for X; likely modest sacrifice for Y.

Put yourself in for "Y." Would you donate your organ to an "X" who was a stranger or a casual acquaintance? There are people who have done that. Dorothy Day, if organ donation had been perfected back in her day, might have given her kidney to some needy person in one of the shelters where she worked. I myself have no inclination whatsoever to become a live donor to a stranger. If you do, then, God bless you, you're a better person than I am.

Now put someone you love dearly in as the donor "Y." Given what you've learned so far from me about Bill Miller, what would you say to your loved one if Bill Miller were "X"? Would you say, *Don't do it! Why think Bill will take good enough care of your kidney that giving it to him will do him significant good?* That's what I would have said if one of my sons had contemplated donating a kidney to Bill. I would have added, "I know he's your uncle, but he never even sent you a birthday card when you were a kid."

However, my Lenten question was not whether to give a kidney to a stranger or what I would say to one of my sons. My Lenten question was: *Am I, this very person that I am, willing to give Bill, this very brother that I have, my kidney?*

For years, I had been praying daily for Bill's restoration. For years, I had ended every phone call with him by saying, "I love you," wanting that to be the last thing he heard from me no matter how long his journey lasted. I wanted to mean what I prayed and mean what I said to him. When I asked myself, *Is risking my own health a reasonable trade-off for restoring my brother's health?* that question seemed too much like asking, *Whose life is worth more, his or mine?* Answering *Mine is!* seemed far from loving.

Still, I had no illusions about whether getting a new kidney would turn Bill into a different person. When I pictured our posttransplant futures, I saw him being almost as miserable on antirejection drugs as he had been on dialysis. And I suspected that I would watch his spotty compliance with what transplant recipients should do with as much dismay as I'd watched his spotty compliance as a dialysis patient.

But here's the thing: I was unwilling to be a person who would tell her brother that she valued her own comfort more highly than his life. I needed us both to know that I valued him enough to give him my kidney.

When I entered the kidney donor application process, I knew that the underbelly of that decision was some murky need. At the time, I suspected I simply needed to think well of myself. But in hindsight, I see my need as somehow entwined with the mystery of family.

My husband, Steve, knows who his people are. Steve's mother was Norwegian on both sides, his father's father Romanian, his father's mother Finnish. Culturally, my mother-in-law's large extended Norwegian American family overwhelmed her husband's mix of Romanian and Finnish, partly because he was an only child of parents who both died before he was twenty-five. Grace had taken Virg's last name, but Virg became a member of Grace's tribe. The customs and stories that shaped Steve's childhood were from Norway. How Bestamama's family lit their Christmas tree with live candles and muttered *uff da* instead of heck.

With my mother a mix and my father in his own odd way undocumented, at some point over the first decades of our marriage, Steve's people became my people. I made *kringle* for every birthday. We followed Steve's family ritual of a Christmas "almond prize," hiding a blanched almond in rice pudding and then awarding a prize to the person who finds it in his or her bowl. I learned to make *berlinerkranser*. My transformation to quasi-Norwegian happened early enough that, if asked, our sons would name their ancestry as Norwegian without a sense of leaving anything of importance out.

Philosophers tell a story called "The Ship of Theseus" that generates perplexities about persistence of objects through time. The story comes from Plutarch. The ancient Greek hero Theseus had a ship that the Greeks wanted to preserve because of its fame. Any time a plank rotted they replaced it with a sturdy new board. Eventually, none of the original planks remained. Plutarch reports that Greek philosophers were divided on the question whether the ship is or is not the one that carried Theseus across the sea. Does Carol Miller still exist if she's become so thoroughly a Simon that her sons are unaware of what "Miller" amounts to, beyond a name she used to have?

On the classic version of *Star Trek* that I watched as a kid, a device called a transporter beamed people from one place to another by dissolving them and reconstituting them somewhere else. I remember an episode where a transporter malfunction resulted in people being neither here nor there. Or did they arrive elsewhere but were no longer themselves? Early on, the tug toward Simon-hood felt like dislocation. But over time, Simon-hood—so vivid, so uncomplicated—beamed me up.

Over the last several years, my frequent conversations with Bill had been reconstituting my Miller-hood, but it ached like a limb withered through neglect. In one of Jesus's healings, he tells a man with a withered hand, "Stretch out your hand." As soon as the man does what Jesus tells him, his hand is restored. Offering my kidney to Bill was a way of stretching out my withered Miller-hood. Antoine de Saint-Exupéry is right: Fraternity is the creation of sacrifices. There is a rare use of *brother* as a verb. One brothers someone—makes him one's brother—by treating him as a brother. By entering the kidney donation program on Bill's behalf toward the end of Lent in 2017, I was brothering Bill. I was treating both our siblinghood and my Miller-hood as more than biological accidents.

When I told Bill that I'd applied to be his donor, he said, "Listen, if we're not a match, don't let them talk you into doing that indirect match thing. That's just a scam." I didn't comment on that, but I could hear relief and joy in Bill's voice.

Not long after that, Bill told me that he had started drinking again. "I've cut way back. I deserve to celebrate occasionally." He went on to explain that teetotaling was not a requirement for staying on the kidney transplant list. In response to my silence, he continued, "Don't worry. I'm not going to end up some homeless alcoholic on skid row."

Bill's drinking frustrated me but did not tempt me to reconsider. I had no stomach for trying to barter my kidney for my brother's sobriety.

After weeks had passed, someone from the transplant center called me. "We appreciate your willingness to be a donor. It's wonderful that you want to do that. Unfortunately, your history of high blood pressure disqualifies you," she said.

I was surprised. As part of the medical history in the application, I'd disclosed that I was on medications to control my blood pressure. I had been taking them since college, but my BP has always been well controlled. It had not occurred to me that such a small thing would preclude getting to the next stage of the physical examinations, blood work, and other tests.

"Will you be telling my brother, or should I?" I asked.

"Well, your application process is confidential. What you share about it with others is up to you."

As I hung up, I felt heaviness with an underside of relief, as if I was in the aftermath of a long cry. I sat for a few minutes looking toward the window. Turning my attention back to my work seemed both impossible and distasteful. I got up. As I passed my assistant's office I said, "Gretchen, I'm going out for a walk. I'll be back in time for my next appointment."

That evening, I called Bill. "Well," he said. We both waited in a long pause that felt like a held breath. "Well," he began again, "I wouldn't want a kidney that wasn't in good shape." Our conversation must have moved on from there. I do not remember what came next.

If I'd been green-lighted all the way through the organ donor process, would I have opted out at some future point? I strive to be resolute, but I do not always succeed. Once Steve and I took our sons, then teenagers, to an amusement park in Ohio called Cedar Point, which was famed for its rollercoasters. I reneged on riding the Millennium Force with them. We'd done the Raptor and the Corkscrew earlier that day. I got into line with them, intending to go. About a half hour into our wait, I began to feel physically queasy. The longer we waited, the higher the three-hundred-foot-high Millennium Force looked. I think I would have gotten on, maybe even enjoyed the thrill, if the wait had been shorter. But as it was, I turned back, excusing myself as I squeezed by the scores of people in line behind us.

In the case of the donor process, Bill's hopefulness would have increased at each hoop I made it through. Yanking that away from him would have been appalling. I expect—I hope—that I would have gone through with it, no matter what level my apprehension reached. But I'll never know.

"No single event can awaken within us a stranger totally unknown to us," says Antoine de Saint-Exupéry. Neither Bill nor I were transformed by my decision to apply to become his donor. Yet perhaps it changed each of us subtlety. "To live is to be slowly born."

CHAPTER 11

Bouts of Fragility

I was surprised to see my boss, Beck Taylor, standing outside Weyerhaeuser Hall in his Brooks Brothers overcoat as two EMTs wheeled my gurney along the slushy sidewalk. Beck had left the building thirty minutes earlier after our usual two-and-a-half-hour president's cabinet meeting ended. I wondered who had told him.

During the first two hours of that president's cabinet meeting in January 2018, I felt fine. Then I began having what I'd come to think of as a "spell." I associated the feeling with fainting couches and sickly Victorian heroines, though I didn't feel like I was about to faint. I felt like I was about to die. I had not mentioned the spells to anyone, not even Steve. They didn't happen often, and up until that day, I had successfully waited them out by breathing slowly and drinking sips of water.

The spells began during our trip to visit our son Matt's family at Thanksgiving. That visit had the added joy of meeting our newest granddaughter, Skyler Reece, for the first time. She'd been born in June. I did not want to spoil that joy with illness, so on the Friday after Thanksgiving, as our older granddaughter Riley played in the jumpy houses at an arcade where we'd taken her, I repeatedly excused myself to the restroom where I could do my deep breathing privately.

I spent the last half hour of the cabinet meeting in an internal debate about whether to excuse myself. I felt I should leave, but I did not want to disrupt the meeting. So, I sat there, willing myself to remain upright, hoping the spell would pass. By the time the meeting concluded, I wasn't sure I could make it to the doorway, let alone across campus to my office. I leaned over to the colleague sitting next to me and told her I was feeling unwell.

"What do you need? What can I do?" she asked.

"I'm not sure. I feel so peculiar."

"Should I call 911?"

I thought about that for a few minutes before nodding yes.

Soon two firefighters—Spokane's first responders—folded into the mix of people in the room, followed by two EMTs. I tried to keep my answers to their flow of questions crisp and accurate. The EMTs stood by while a fireman took my vitals. Oxygen level good. Blood pressure and heart rate elevated. Finally, one of the firemen asked, *Do you want someone to drive you to the Emergency Room or do you want to be taken by ambulance?*

What would you recommend?

It's your call. If it were me, I'd take the ambulance.

So off I went. As the EMTs wheeled me along, I felt like an extra in a movie, someone playing "woman on a gurney." Beck, standing stiffly with his hands in his pockets near the ambulance, looked like he'd been cast as a one-man honor guard. At any moment, he might salute. Instead, he looked down at me long enough to make eye contact, then nodded and shifted his gaze off to the side. He wished what I wished—that neither of us were there right now.

The EMTs lifted me. I gave Beck a thumbs up, before the gurney slid into the ambulance.

In the ambulance, there's continual radio chatter that doesn't seem to have anything to do with those on board. The woman on the gurney tunes it out so she can listen to what the man sitting inches from her is saying. Sometimes he explains to her what he's doing. *Inserting an IV in case it's needed. Hooking you to the monitor now.* Sometimes he speaks to someone at the hospital.

What can she do but nod as the attendant explains what he's doing? What can she do but let them drive her down Division Street even though she always takes Country Homes instead? She hates Division's four lanes of congestion, the ugly sameness of its big box stores, fast-food franchises, pawn shops, and drive-through espresso stands.

She finds that she's acquired strange powers. Cars are pulling over and stopping, making way for them—for her—as if she were Moses, and the traffic were the sea. She senses precisely when they pass Division Street's few distinctive places: Bigfoot Tavern, then Tomato Street Italian restaurant, then the sculpture of the leaping salmon near the convention center. But by the time she finds herself in an examining room, in a hospital gown, hooked up to monitors, she's become a cork afloat in the flow of the hospital's routines. A man staring at a laptop types in her answers to the same questions she's answered many times this day.

Twice she's wheeled down the hallway to other places. Once to have a chest X-ray. Once to have a CAT scan of her head. Each time she's returned to the same examination room, where her husband sits waiting, reading news feeds on his cell phone. "How are you feeling, sweetie?" he asks. Except for the odd, timeless passivity arising from hours of being shuffled through corridors on a gurney, she now feels fine.

The attendant—intern? resident?—has been in and out. He returns. After looking at the laptop screen for several minutes, he says that they have no explanation for what the woman on the gurney reported feeling. No heart attack. No stroke.

Have you been especially anxious lately? he asks. Last semester, she suspects as part of get-out-the-vote efforts in the upcoming midterm elections, she had been pummeled with emails and phone calls for weeks. A student connected to a local chapter of a national organization had written an opinion piece in the student newspaper claiming that textbooks used in Whitworth courses promoted immoral views. His editorial was posted on the national organization's website along with her contact information. She considers all there's been to be anxious about—politics, mass shootings, natural disasters, tight university budgets, and intradepartmental squabbles. Through it all, the woman on the gurney was calmer than most people she knows. She shrugs and shakes her head no.

Sometimes this happens, he says, mirroring her shrug. *You should call your primary care doctor and see her within the next day or two. Good luck to you.*

I waited a few days after the ambulance ride—my first—to tell Bill about it. I did not want Bill to be overly worried about me. In the three and a half years since his health crisis began, he had had enough problems of his own to worry about. I framed the incident as a joke on myself. My having to grapple with doctors now created shared ground that we had not had before.

Many days I felt completely normal all day. Some days, I would feel fine for hours but then the fragile feeling would creep up on me. One evening when Steve was out somewhere, I lay down on the couch. My body felt like it was having some massive but diffuse systemic failure. Dying seemed like a real and imminent possibility, but a possibility that caused me no distress for my own sake. As I lay there, I began to think about how awful it would be for Steve to come home and find me dead. I was still lying there when Steve came home, but I had begun to feel somewhat better.

"Should we go to urgent care?" he asked. I told him I'd go see the doctor the next day but for now I was going to bed.

It took another several weeks before I was able to identify eating gluten-rich foods as a possible trigger for my spells. Gluten intolerance, which undermines the intestine's ability to absorb nutrients, explained the anemia that one of my doctors had diagnosed. When I cut gluten out of my diet, the spells stopped. I felt better than I had for quite some time. I realized that my system had been like the proverbial frog in the pot of water gradually being heated to a boil. I hadn't noticed the gradual onslaught of unwellness until the situation became acute.

Those months of feeling like my body was unreliable gave me an inkling of what Bill had been experiencing for years, but no more than an inkling. My bout of fragility was like being trapped in an elevator for a few hours; his experience as a dialysis patient was more like spending unending time under a shifting pile of rubble.

Simone Weil invites us to focus on how prone our bodies are to injury and disease, how vulnerable our souls are in the face of depression, how illusory our social status is. Weil recommends pondering our almost infinite fragility wherever we experience joy. Awareness of joy's fragility will increase its piercing sweetness. She reminds us that cherry blossoms are more beautiful for being frail.

For years I have wondered about my calmness during those months that I periodically felt I was dying. It reminded me of Emily Dickinson's "formal feeling," which she said comes after pain. What was it? Serenity? Disbelief? Numb resignation? I do not know. What I do know is that it was nothing like affliction. Odd that feeling on death's verge could feel like affliction's antipole.

A year before all this transpired, Steve and I began making time during visits to our son Matt's family to drive around neighborhoods near the Charlotte suburb where they lived. Occasionally, we stopped to look through homes with open house signs in their yards. Neither Steve nor I had any strong desire to live in the South. But we had seen what our sons and their grandparents had missed out on by living hundreds of miles from each other. We did not want to repeat that pattern with our granddaughters.

My "spells" nudged me to begin thinking about a timeline for rounding off my work at Whitworth. I wanted to retire close to my peak and avoid being one of those provosts who left behind the smell of week-old fish in people's memories.

Given Bill's situation and my mother-in-law's decline, we valued being within driving distance of Portland. Though we were not shy about talking with Steve's siblings about our tentative plans to move to Charlotte sometime in the next few years, I avoided bringing up the topic with Bill. I felt queasy about whether even the possibility of our moving so far away would feel like abandonment to him. His life seemed always on the verge of unraveling. How could I be on call to help him reweave his life if I were more than a forty-five-minute plane trip away?

CHAPTER 12

Pulling Away

By the time you know connections are fraying, sometimes they are beyond mending. One moment, the fabric looks fine, the next, there is a rip. When patched, the fabric pulls away in another place, making a worse tear.

In 2018, one thread holding us in the Pacific Northwest broke more suddenly than we'd expected. Six months after my ambulance ride, Steve's sister Sherry called to say their mom was under hospice care in her apartment at The Springs. That was not a surprise. We knew that Sherry had gone to Portland to help their sister Katie set that up. What surprised us was Sherry saying it would be a good idea for Steve to come right away. His mom had taken a turn the day before. The staff did not give her much time.

Sherry called a few hours later to tell us Mom was dead. Steve had not even had time to book a flight.

Steve and I last saw Mom the April before she died. By then she'd been in a wheelchair for two years, which was just as well. Her weak legs meant she could stay in her assisted living apartment instead of being locked away in The Spring's memory unit.

During that visit, the three of us looked through a photo book that Matt and Julie had given Mom with pictures of her great-granddaughter Riley. On some days Mom seemed to understand, but that day she kept asking, "Whose baby is that now?" As the three of us sat at her small dining room table, she kept reaching out to touch the same flower in the bouquet of miniature yellow roses we had brought her. "So pretty," she'd say. Then "I like your shoes," looking down at my feet. Then, "So pretty" again as her finger grazed the flower's petals. Then "I like your shoes."

"She didn't know who we were," Steve said afterward, shaking his head as if shooing away the thought.

"The flowers made her happy," I said. "Still enjoying things, that's something."

"I won't come," Bill said, when I called to tell him they'd scheduled Mom's memorial service for the Saturday after she died. "I don't have anything but sweatpants and gym shorts to wear."

"Oh, please come. Grace would have wanted you there. We're coming down on Tuesday. I can take you shopping on Thursday." Bill wouldn't have dialysis that day.

Bill had last seen Grace two years before she died, at the party that her children had arranged for her ninetieth birthday. It had been a small group, less than a dozen close family members. She wore a rhinestone tiara that Sherry had bought her and a vacant smile.

When I took Bill to the department store, we started our shopping with shirts. Then we looked at slacks but found none short enough in Bill's waist size. Always stocky, he used to be solid. Now his belly had become like exuberant bread dough. Seeing that Bill was losing energy, I walked him over to a dressing room and left him to try on the shirts.

Pawing through my fourth pile of men's Bermuda shorts. I came to a light tan pair with a waist size that might work for Bill's distended abdomen. I put the shorts over my arm and continued the search, hoping that having choices would lessen Bill's discouragement. On my way back to Bill's dressing room, I spotted a rack of shorts I had not looked through. I found a light blue pair with the right waist size.

As I handed the tan and blue shorts over the top of the dressing room door, I asked, "How did the shirts work?"

"Two of them are decent."

Bill came out of the dressing room, saying that he'd take the tan shorts and both shirts. He looked spent. I told him to sit in the chair next to the dressing room while I went to pay for the clothes and drive the car up to the curb. I wished, not for the first time, that Bill would put practicality before pride and use his walker.

Three minutes before the service was supposed to start, Bill arrived wearing the darker of the shirts we had found—brown with a subtle suggestion of bamboo-like foliage. He looked fine, despite the shorts, I thought. In the Pacific Northwest people show up dressed all sorts of ways—even for funerals.

We walked into the back of the chapel together. I expected that he'd join me in sitting by Paul and Matt, who had flown in the day before, in the left front pew. Instead, Bill slid into a pew further back—the first one he came to that had an empty seat on the aisle.

The service Steve conducted was brief. A few remembrances, but no music, no singing. Steve had felt unable to do the homily at his dad's service. His grief in that instance was too raw. But he began grieving his mother years before her death, when she'd stopped being able to remember his birthday.

Steve and I spent the next hour and a half circulating among the attendees at the reception on the patio outside the chapel. Bill filled a plate of food and sat down at a table off to the side, alone. I went into the bar and ordered two glasses of white wine, setting one down by his plate and wandering off with the other. Every few minutes, I'd walk over to where he was sitting. Occasionally, someone would come by his table while I was there, and I'd introduce them to Bill. Though he did not seem to be enjoying himself, he lingered.

At one point, Paul and Matt sat down at Bill's table. Both my sons had shed their sport coats and loosened their ties. Whenever I would glance their way, the three of them looked pleasantly occupied. One of them had brought Bill a second glass of wine. He'd last seen his nephews two years earlier, when we'd rented an Airbnb house in Portland's West Hills for a family reunion.

I went over and asked Paul and Matt to lean toward Bill so I could take their picture. That turned out to be the last time my sons saw their Uncle Bill, though not through my lack of trying.

Steve's mother had wanted her ashes mingled with her husband's and scattered somewhere on the Oregon coast. We found a tour boat operator in Depoe Bay who would take families three miles offshore, where scattering ashes was allowed. We made a reservation for a date in June of 2019, eighteen months after she died, and reserved a beach house that would sleep up to twelve adults. Our sons' families and all our siblings would come for a family reunion during which a smaller contingent would scatter Virg and Grace's ashes.

Initially, Bill seemed enthusiastic about joining us. He talked with his dialysis center, and they arranged for him to receive two treatments at an affiliated center twenty minutes from where we would be staying on the coast. But three days before the gathering, Bill reconsidered.

"There're only two techs at my facility that know what they are doing," he said. "The others poke me like I'm a pin cushion. I don't want to deal with some rookie at a center I've never used."

Bill had done something similar six months before, when the plan was for him to come with Steve's siblings, Katie and John, to our house for three days at Christmas. Katie would drive and the three of them would split the cost of gas. Steve and I were looking forward to the opportunity to host our siblings for a holiday. But ten days before Christmas, Bill told me he had changed his mind. "I don't think I can take hours of Katie's nonstop talking in the car," he said.

The timing of his decision put me in a bind. I intended to finish my Christmas shopping that coming weekend. Now, to get Bill's presents to him by Christmas, I'd need to ship them before then. My schedule for the next few days was packed with Whitworth work and evening events.

Steve had a down vest someone had given him last Christmas that he had worn once, maybe twice. It was extra large, stylish, and useful. The kind of thing we might have taken with us to Portland had Bill try on, giving it to him if he decided he wanted it. I put the vest in a Macy's box we had on hand and wrapped it, along with other things I had already bought Bill for Christmas. The shipping cost for such a bulky box was more than the vest would have cost new, but I told myself it was worth it because it would give Bill something big to open.

Early in January, Bill called me. "I tried returning that vest you sent to Macy's. They wouldn't take it back. No tags. Not even a brand they carry, they said. They made me feel like I was trying to put something over on them."

Bill's story sat there between us. How could I explain that something that now seemed unthinkable had seemed thoughtful to me at the time? It made no sense—not even to me. Looking back, I am tempted to psychoanalyze my actions as passive-aggressive payback for his having backed out of coming for Christmas. Given the essay prompt "Write about something shameful you've done," this vignette would be what I'd write. I sent him a check for a hundred dollars with a note: *Buy something you like.*

Was Bill pulling out of coming to Depoe Bay his own passive-aggressive payback for my Christmas blunder? I did not ask—I am a Miller, after all; Millers do not ask. But the thought that Bill might have taken my sending him a Christmas-wrapped hand-me-down as some message makes me heartsick.

I thought at the time that Bill just didn't care enough about family to make the effort, but I had no idea, really, how much effort anything took for him, especially on dialysis days. Nor did I have any idea what exposing his decrepitude to his nephews and their families felt like. He might have viewed excusing himself to do dialysis, then recuperating from it with others around, as humiliating. Back when Bill had come to a similar Simon family gathering we hosted near Cannon Beach two years before his health crisis, he rode his motorcycle over the coastal range. The contrast might have been too painful for him to bear. The afflicted, Simone Weil tells us, experience the same shivering horror when faced with themselves as anyone does when they see death in its nakedness, not dressed up.

Or there's this possibility: Just before that gathering at the Oregon coast, Steve and I made an offer on a house in the Carolinas. It was in a neighborhood we'd been scouting fifteen minutes from Matt and Julie's. We made an offer significantly lower than the asking price. To our surprise, the owners accepted. Steve and I made plans to retire the following June and move to the new house sometime after that. I don't now remember whether I told Bill about the Carolina house before or after he decided not to come to Depoe Bay. But if it was before, Bill may have thought it was I who did not care enough.

Or here's another guess: It must have been around this time that Bill told me he had been removed from the kidney transplant list. I again do not remember how the timeline went. I do remember that when he was removed from the list, Bill blamed his cardiologist for expressing her opinion that his heart would not tolerate the surgery. "She should have just not written a letter if she couldn't be positive," he insisted.

For the three years he was on the list, Bill underwent extensive annual reevaluations. Each time he assumed people were looking for excuses to take him off the list. Failure to requalify, he thought, would confirm that his life was deemed less worthy than others. No amount of reassurance from me convinced him otherwise.

Simone Weil reminds us that "Why?" has two meanings: "By what cause?" and "For what purpose?" The afflicted person who asks, "Why am I afflicted?" wants to know the purpose, not the causes, of his condition. I heard my sister Diana's pleas of "I've been good. I've been good" as she lay dying as implied questions: "Why me? What's this for?" I think my mother's comment that God had experienced the death of a Son, not a daughter was also a tacit "Why?" *Why my daughter? Why so young?*

Why questions only point us in the right direction if we ask them persistently and don't settle for cheap, made-up answers. The real answers, Weil tells us, lie beyond this world.

Weil implies that asking "Why?" in the face of suffering is not just natural, but sacred, for what is sacred in every human heart is the expectation that good and not evil will be done to us. Yet Weil also says that the afflicted "become impotent in using language because of the certitude that they are not heard." The sacred part of the afflicted is not dead, but mute. I have often wondered whether Bill reached such a point.

Weil also tells us that affliction stamps the soul with contempt, disgust, and self-hatred. It fosters a sense of guilt and defilement. I find it horrible to think that the reason I never heard my brother ask, "Why me?" is that he'd stopped believing that he was worthy of asking.

It's quite possible that Bill did not want to connect with his extended family because he was simply overwhelmed, depressed, and ground down. Things that I was too distracted to see—or too self-centered to want to see.

So many questions that Bill alone could answer. Questions it is too late now to ask.

CHAPTER 13

Smells of Childhood

It was December 2019 when Bill told me, "The thrill is gone." An ominous sign. For years now, Bill had put the middle of his hand over a long, wide scar on his left arm each day to check for a vibration—the thrill—that indicated blood was flowing through his arteriovenous fistula. No thrill indicated an obstruction that would make the fistula useless for dialysis.

Five years earlier a doctor had gerrymandered Bill's circulatory system by connecting a vein to an artery. Since then, a technician had poked two long needles into the fistula over five hundred times. One of those two needles connected to a tube through which his blood was pumped out and into the dialysis machine, the other to a tube that returned Bill's filtered blood to his body. Bill's fistular vein, having suffered the insult of being poked once too often, had collapsed.

A temporary plastic access was inserted near Bill's clavicle so he could continue dialysis while awaiting surgery to construct a new fistula. "Not exactly a chick magnet," Bill said, repeating his complaint from five years earlier about the device protruding near his neck. The weariness in his voice undercut his attempt to make light of this setback.

I flew to Portland from San Diego the day after a vascular surgeon constructed Bill's new fistula, so I could help with wound care and provide moral support. I was coming from the January 2020 Whitworth Board of Trustees' Retreat. The historic Hotel del Coronado, built in the nineteenth century, was a picturesque setting for our meetings but struck my boss, Beck, and the trustees as too threadbare for habitation. They had opted to stay in The Views, a modern building, with floor-to-ceiling windows and spacious bathrooms, that was part of the hotel's complex. I'd seen the trustees only in meetings or near the beach at the open-air Tiki Bar with its thatched roof. I and the rest of Whitworth's staff were staying in the historic hotel, where the bathrooms were cramped, windows small, and wooden floors wavy with age.

Even when descending from Spokane into Bill's ramshackle life, the contrast between the ample orderliness of my everyday life and what I encountered there always made me uneasy. Coming to Bill's from the board retreat, where I'd eaten lavish dinners after watching the sun set over the ocean, was more disorienting. Though my room at the Hotel del Coronado had been deemed too shabby to house a trustee, it had been larger and considerably cleaner than my brother's whole apartment. Though I was in Portland for Bill's sake, there was no place for me to sleep at Bill's. I was sleeping at my sister-in-law Katie's house across town.

As I stood in Bill's small kitchen, I could easily talk to him across the breakfast bar as he sat watching TV in his recliner only a few feet away. Occasionally, Bill would move to the small desk and ask his cat, Willy, if he wanted to be brushed. Willy would jump up onto the desk and the two of them would lock their eyes. Bill, a relaxed smile lighting his face, slowly stroked the cat's swaying body. It pleased me to watch this ritual as I peeled potatoes, carrots, and onions to cook with the pot roast Bill requested. Our mother had made pot roast for most Sunday midday dinners, browning the meat, then cooking it and the vegetables on low in an electric fry pan while we were at church. For several hours Bill's apartment smelled like our childhood.

Bill and I ate our dinner off plates balanced on our laps—he had no space for a dining room table. Afterwards, I'd put the rest of the roast and vegetables into dinner-portioned containers, to freeze along with the chicken breasts and pork loin I'd cooked.

Before I left, I changed the dressing on Bill's arm. The raw tenderness of Bill's new fistula moved me. How could its strangeness have come to seem mundane? Are there practices more grotesque than creating a wound, letting it heal into a scar, and then stabbing it with needles to pump a person's lifeblood through a machine? Yet this grotesquery had kept Bill alive for over five years.

By my third day in Portland, I'd filled Bill's freezer, so I asked him if there was any place he wanted to go on my remaining day in Portland. Bill's answer was Cannon Beach, on the Oregon coast. He had not been out of Portland since he'd been able to ride his Harley-Davidson down Highway 101.

If we were going to spend time on the coast, I wanted to get Bill near the surf. Searching online, I found a place that rented wheelchairs with large tires for beach use. Bill said thanks, but no.

Part of me understood why Bill did not want to subject himself to conspicuous decrepitude, though I hope I will always be willing to suffer humiliation to be near waves crashing on the shore. A picture I keep on my bedside table of our mother shows her left arm resting on a cane strapped to her forearm with Velcro. Her other cane is resting against the wooden deck rail behind her. Beyond the deck is a long stretch of beach and Pacific Ocean waves battering two large rocky outcroppings characteristic of the northern Oregon coast. At the time of the picture, Mom's eyesight was dimmed with macular degeneration, but she could hear the ocean's rhythms and inhale its pungency. The picture shows our mother's hard-earned serenity. She looks like she is gazing into eternity, a hint of a smile on her face.

As I drove toward the coast on Highway 26, Bill sat beside me with his left arm propped on a pillow and said little until we passed the section of mountains that in our childhood memories were denuded by the Tillamook Burn. He commented on how tall and dense the firs and hemlocks had become. I asked, "Do you remember that old restaurant we used to stop at when we were kids? The one called Pixie Kitchen?" Bill nodded but lapsed back into silence.

On the outskirts of Cannon Beach, I turned off Highway 101 into Ecola State Park. The road narrowed as switchbacks took us higher at each turn. The road ended at a parking lot where, several yards down a path, the Ecola Point overlook promised a panorama. There was only one other car in the lot on this chilly January morning. The path was paved. I offered to get the walker out of the trunk, but Bill said he'd stay in the car. Only in hindsight do I realize that he'd likely been advised not to do anything that would stress his healing fistula.

I walked past shrubs still dripping from an earlier drizzle. The sky held a high overcast, but the air below the viewpoint was clear enough to see Haystack Rock rising above low fog three miles away. The ocean churning around nearby basalt outcroppings produced a beat that sent ". . .vast, unmeasured, boundless, free. . ." looping through my mind. I stayed for only a few minutes, not wanting Bill to be sitting alone in the car too long.

As we made our way through the town of Cannon Beach, I kept looking for a place where I'd be able to get Bill a direct outdoor view of the ocean, where he could hear the surf and smell the brine. I turned down a side street that dead-ended at a railing on the top of a retaining wall, with the beach many feet below. Bill took his time getting out of the car, but soon both of us were standing at the railing with the breeze in our faces. A stiff breeze had blown away the fog. We could see breakers a long way out.

As we stood there, I asked him if he remembered the time that Mom had driven onto the beach's shingle—which in Oregon is legal—and the car got stuck. My mother had Bill, Diana, and me get out and stand at a safe distance while she reversed, then went forward, reversed, then went forward, again and again, rocking the car gently until it made a path for itself and regained traction. She'd mastered this technique, which requires patience and persistence, in Michigan snow.

Bill's reaction was unreadable. I could not tell whether being here mattered to him. Perhaps he was just indulging me.

We got back in the car and drove on to Mo's, a restaurant whose big windows provide a beach-level view of the ocean and Haystack. As Bill ate fried oysters and I ate a shrimp salad, we watched people walking, hooded heads down. Near Haystack's base, some people stooped to peer into tide pools, as I remembered doing many times over the years. I handed Bill my phone and he scrolled through the pictures I'd taken from the Ecola Park overlook. Though he ate with a surprising appetite for a dialysis patient, he gave no signs of pleasure at the view.

After lunch, we stopped at the candy store Bill remembered. The place was busy. As Bill took his time deciding what he wanted, I admired the friendly artistry of the women in dark blue aprons scooping candy into small white paper bags. Bill chose three different kinds of chocolates. I got some red licorice to take back to Spokane for Steve, and a few chocolates for my sister-in-law and me to share that evening.

As Bill and I stepped out of the store, I saw large bronze sculptures of animals in the window of an art gallery next door and asked Bill if he'd like to go in. He shrugged. "If you want." After only a few minutes, Bill sat down on a leather couch, saying, "Don't rush on my account." I looked at a few more paintings and sculptures without being able to take them in. Bill's impatience seemed to waft toward me from behind.

As we got back into the car, I asked Bill if there was anything else he wanted to do. "That's enough," he said, "let's head home."

It was a stunted and misshapen day—for me, as it must have been for Bill. Yet my memory of it contains an element of beauty, like that of the wind-sculpted coastal pines that cling to coastal cliffs. I hope in the mix of all that Bill was feeling and not saying, there was something akin to that for him as well.

CHAPTER 14

Dusty Guest Room

The day I returned to Whitworth after visiting Bill on my way home from the trustees' retreat, I needed to settle a dispute between our director of off-campus programs and a history professor. The historian was angry because he was scheduled to speak at a conference in China in February and the off-campus programs director was saying that he should not go. There was an outbreak of a virus in a place called Wuhan, which was five hundred miles from where the conference was being held. The faculty member thought the program director had no business telling him what to do. Yet it was, in fact, part of the director's job to apply the university's policy about US State Department advisories to faculty professional travel. I sided with the director, though I agreed with the faculty member that going would not have involved much risk. Little did I know.

The Wuhan virus spread like uncontainable wildfire. By the end of February, the governor of Washington declared a statewide health emergency. Knowing that the stay-at-home order was coming, I extended Whitworth's usual one-week spring break to two weeks to give faculty time to transition their courses to an online format. Students were told to take all their textbooks and course materials with them when they left campus. I formed a team within the academic area, headed by one of my deans who had internet savvy, to provide training on a variety of online platforms. On March 23rd, the governor issued a stay-at-home order.

My last four months as Whitworth's provost went by in a haze of decision fatigue and Zoom meetings spaced so closely in time that, on some days, bathroom breaks felt like a luxury. Education continued to happen at Whitworth, with many creative accommodations. On the fly we had to answer such questions as: What does an online student-teacher placement look like for an elementary education major? An online nursing practicum? An online chemistry lab? We were feeling our way into those questions, and most of what we did felt yucky.

Few things are more debilitating to someone who cares about teaching well than to be doing a passable job of the impossible. None of us, really, wanted to settle for *it wasn't a complete waste of time* or *she did the best she could.* But what we wanted had little to do with what we were called on to do.

As the semester came to its close, some of my Zoom meetings were with my successor, providing him with an overview of the situation he was to inherit. Celebrations of my retirement were also held via Zoom. Beck Taylor came to my house one day to deliver the Bulova mantel clock with its "In Gratitude" engraved plate. We sat on my patio six feet apart, face-to-face, and unmasked for the first time in weeks.

Simone Weil gives a long list of distorted ways to minister to those in affliction. If we address their needs capriciously, or irregularly, or from vanity or pity, or so that our conscience will be clear, our gifts will be an injury. Our tactless sympathy will make the afflicted person feel like a specimen—like exhibit A in the display case of affliction or an item to be checked off a to-do list. As the afflicted experience repeated inept gestures of help, they stop voicing their needs, even to themselves. Simone Weil tells us, "Each afflicted being, under the constraint of general indifference, tries either by lying or unconsciousness to make himself deaf to himself."

It is so hard for the afflicted to preserve their self-respect that Weil claims that this only happens supernaturally. Oh, Bill, I pray that God gave you that help.

Bill's existence during the first six months of the pandemic was a strange mix of risk and relative safety. Three days a week, he spent four hours near others, but everyone in the dialysis facility wore medical-grade masks, had their temperature checked before entry, and were tested weekly for COVID once tests were available.

Bill avoided COVID, but in May he suffered with a stubborn case of MRSA, an antibiotic-resistant staph infection. The boils on his skin were painful and, as the infection dragged on, his fear of having to be hospitalized added a layer of psychological pain. He was convinced that if he went into the hospital or an inpatient care facility, he would catch COVID and die. After a few weeks, his doctor succeeded in finding a drug combination that cured his MRSA.

COVID had taken any attraction out of the idea of living half the year in Spokane, half in the Carolinas. We planned to move in late summer or early fall, depending on how quickly our Spokane house sold. We debated whether to wait until the pandemic ended before moving but decided to forge ahead. Before we put the house on the market, we wanted to go to Portland, if our family members there were willing to take the risk of our visiting.

I called Bill and said we were planning on coming. Steve and I had not eaten at a restaurant since February, but I knew that Bill had dined in one a few times when isolation got too much for him to bear. I said we'd either bring take-out food to his apartment or, if he wanted to find a place with outdoor seating, we'd take him to a restaurant.

The second day we were in Portland, Steve and I went to Bill's apartment to pick him up for a midday dinner. Looking around, I understood why Bill had chosen to have us take him out. Every inch of the kitchen's counter space was filled with pill bottles, dishes, cat food, and small appliances. If I'd been there on my own, I'd have tried to do some cleaning. But I suspected that Bill would not want his brother-in-law as an audience to his sister's dissing his housekeeping. I emptied Little Willy's litter box and took Bill's trash down to the dumpster as we left but let the rest of the mess be. Bill walked slowly down the hallway to the elevator and across the parking lot to our car. By the time he got in, he was winded.

Steve dropped us at the entrance of the roadhouse that Bill had chosen and went to park the car. The waitress politely tried to match Bill's slow pace as we crossed the large, almost-empty dining room. We had the restaurant's deck, which overlooked an offshoot of the Willamette River, to ourselves since the temperature was in the low sixties. The river added to the damp chill but provided a soothing background burble and visual distraction. Bill sat at one end of a six-person table, Steve and I together at the other end. After ordering, we took our masks off so we could talk more easily.

It had been a year since Bill and Steve had seen each other. Their usual topic of conversation was sports since they shared little else in common. With sports on hiatus, Steve resorted to telling Bill about the happenings in Reardan, Washington, where he had been an interim pastor for the last eighteen months. He told Bill about the abandoned building on the town's main street that had collapsed of its own weight in the middle of the night. He described how his congregation worshiped on Zoom for several months before resuming in-person worship in his last few weeks there—the masked attendees spread six feet apart in every other pew. Bill seemed to be only half listening as he ate.

I asked Bill when he'd last talked with his friends Pete, Joe, Robin, and Rachel. He said that he and Pete had gotten together for breakfast two week earlier—that Pete's mom had died of COVID and that he'd not been able to be with her when she died. He said that the rest of them seemed to be doing well. Robin and Rachel had stopped by briefly a few weeks earlier.

As we headed out of the restaurant, Steve went ahead to get the car and pull it up to the door. Bill had to stop twice to catch his breath as he and I slowly walked across the dining room to the entrance. When we got to the door, Bill leaned against the wall for a moment to gather his strength. His decline, even compared to how he'd been in January, surprised me.

I'd begun to see Bill in the same category as a man writer Leslie Marmon Silko describes in a letter to her friend James Wright. The man survives one illness and calamity after another—tuberculosis, car accidents, cirrhosis, bullet wounds, pneumonia, cancer of the gums—and becomes famous on Silko's Laguna reservation solely for the fact of being alive. Part of me thought that, come what may, Bill would outlive me, and he'd do that by managing mostly on his own. Yet part of me knew that any given day could be Bill's last.

"Have you thought about what you will do if it gets to a point where it's too hard to live on your own?" I asked.

"Well," he said, "I guess then you'd need to dust off your guest room."

What had I expected him to say? Not that. But how could I have been prepared for Bill staying on a bumpy plateau or falling off a cliff, but not for a downhill slide that would land him in the center of my life? When our mother was using canes and a wheelchair, her youngest sister, Fannie, was diagnosed with scleroderma—a condition where one's skin and other tissues harden. Fannie, like Mom, was a widow. Mom took Fannie in. For four years, they lived together in Mom's double-wide trailer. Though Mom and Fannie traded roles depending on who was doing better on any given day, Mom was the primary caregiver. Here I was, in my mid-sixties, strong and healthy. Could I—would I—do for my brother Bill what Mom did for her sister Fannie?

My mind scrolled through unanswerable questions. How could Bill transition to living with us? What would he do with his time? How would Steve and our dog, Bella, live with Little Willy? What would we talk about for hours on end? On two past occasions, Bill hadn't wanted to use an unfamiliar dialysis center even for one or two rounds of dialysis. How could he cope with a long-term change?

Mind-boggling, even if Steve and I were staying in Spokane, but we were not. The trajectory of our lives seemed set, even though we had not yet sold our house. How would we possibly get Bill to our Charlotte suburb? All those questions flashed through my head as we stood there waiting for Steve to pull up in the car.

I'm fine, Carol. I'll be fine. Do I remember him finally saying that, or is that only what I wished he would have said?

CHAPTER 15

Vigil

Steve and I had just driven out of Washington, embarked on our cross-country move, when Bill called to say that he was back in the hospital. This time he'd been admitted with severe constipation, a side effect of dehydration, which is a side effect of dialysis. "Just wanted you to know. Have a safe journey," he said before hanging up.

Each day I called, Bill sounded more discouraged. Each day I called, I had traveled further away as we made our way to the Carolinas. But by the time we got to our new house, they'd gotten Bill unblocked. "You missed the shit-fest," he said, sounding upbeat.

Steve and I had brought an air mattress, two camp chairs, simple cooking utensils, and a few dishes in the car with us and were camping out in our house as we waited for the moving truck to arrive. The day after our furniture came, I knew there had been a turn in Bill's situation. When I talked to Bill, he told me that he'd decided to give Little Willy to his friend Joe, who'd been taking care of the cat while he was in the hospital. When I called the nurses' station for a medical update, I was told, "Sorry, we do not give out patient information." Up until then, whoever answered had told me about Bill's condition as soon as I introduced myself as "William's" sister.

I offered to email documentation that I had Bill's power of attorney and asked the nurse to have his doctor call me. "I'd recommend you come right away," he said, an echo of another doctor over six years earlier. The doctor told me that Bill had refused surgery to repair his bleeding intestines. Bill wanted no part of ending up with an ostomy bag.

When I told Bill I was coming, he retorted, "What's the point?" Then I heard him yelling at the nurse who was trying to take his blood pressure. "Leave," he shouted. "I said, Get out of here! Sorry, Carol, I can't understand why they won't just leave me the hell alone."

"I'm already ticketed," I said, just as he disconnected.

I took my temperature repeatedly between the time I talked with Bill and the next morning when Steve dropped me at the airport. My throat felt sore, but perhaps I wanted it to be. "Are you sure you're sick?" my mother would ask, frowning, on school days when I felt ill. My temps stayed at 97 degrees or below. I decided to wear two overlapping masks in the airports and on the two legs of the flight.

Bill called as I was reaching the front of the TSA line. He wanted to make sure I knew his room number—the closest he would come to saying that he was glad I was coming.

As I waited for my connecting flight in Dallas, I watched coverage about the wildfires—the worst fire season yet was unfolding across the West. Several new fires had broken out just that morning.

As the plane begins its descent into Portland, my nostrils begin to sting, making me wonder how close the nearest fire is. I am still on East Coast time, my body clock telling me it is well after midnight as I pick up my rental car and drive to the airport Comfort Inn to check in and drop my bag. The desk clerk has no record of my reservation. They are full. My reservation is at the other hotel in their chain, four miles away. This time I don't even take my bag in. I just check in and get my room key. The route between the hotel and the hospital looks like London during its 1950s killer fog. Nothing I pass looks like any place I've ever been. When I get to the hospital, the main entrance is closed. Signs point to an alternative entrance.

Back when I was teaching, I had dreams of walking along unfamiliar corridors, trying to find my classroom—but becoming more confused at every turn in the corridor, my desperation growing, knowing students would be heading to the department office to complain. This would feel like that kind of dream if I weren't too weary to feel.

The side entrance leads into a room where two people sit at a table asking each arrival, "Who are you here to see?" COVID protocols allow only one visitor per patient per day. After I say, "William Miller," the man checks his list, hands me a sheet of COVID screening questions and aims a temperature gun at my forehead. I walk through the metal detector, then make my way through deserted lobbies and hallways. The corridor outside Bill's hospital room would normally be quiet. Instead, exhaust fans fight to clear out the acrid air.

Bill is awake, the head of the bed slightly raised. A dinner tray sits off to the side, its pale soft mounds of food looking untouched. I take Bill's hand, leaning over to give him a kiss, as he raises his head toward me. I ask if he feels up to eating anything.

"There's pudding here. Applesauce," I say, nodding toward his tray.

I help him eat half a container of the pudding.

Simone Weil tells us that a person in affliction quivers like a butterfly pinned alive to a tray. To have one's soul pierced by affliction is equivalent to being nailed to a cross. To be like the good thief hanging beside Jesus at the crucifixion one must acknowledge one's abject need. We become like the impenitent thief if we seek consolation in contempt for others who are experiencing affliction.

Intense, pure attention, without ulterior motives, is a precious gift that we can give to the afflicted, but only through the supernatural operation of grace. According to Weil, "In true love it is not we who love the afflicted in God; it is God in us who loves them. When we are in affliction, it is God in us who loves those who wish us well. Compassion and gratitude come down from God, and when they are exchanged in a glance, God is present at the point where the eyes of those who give and those who receive meet." Though the love between the sufferer and the other starts from God and comes through God, neither is motivated by their love of God. Each loves the other for the other's own sake. Weil says that this is impossible, which is how we know it is supernatural.

Did God give Bill and me that help? I cannot know, but I can hope.

I stayed for perhaps half an hour. I had imagined that, at some point as his death neared, Bill and I would have heartfelt conversations. That I'd be a kind of Lamaze coach in reverse for him, as I'd pictured doing six years earlier when I'd thought he was going to die. Beyond *Sleep well, I love you*, I don't remember what we said.

I get to Bill's room a little after seven. Bill says he's rested well. I choose not to tell him that I did not. We talk haltingly between the usual intrusions of a hospital's morning routine. I leave the room while a nurse helps Bill use a bedpan.

Just before nine, an attendant helps Bill get out of bed and into a chair for the "transition meeting" that the palliative care physician and chaplain have scheduled. The two of them have their script well-rehearsed, but I keep missing my cues. I expected the doctor would be sharing information, laying out options, asking Bill for consent. Instead, the two of them ask Bill oblique questions—*What's been important to you? What have you cared about?* His responses are terse. The answers I supply on his behalf are inane, though he nods agreement: *He likes fixing cars. He enjoys umpiring softball. He loves Thai food.* When they ask whether he wants the chaplain to visit again later in the day, Bill shakes his head no.

As the doctor and chaplain get up to leave, I ask to speak to the doctor in the hallway. I assume Bill will be transitioning out of the hospital to hospice and want her to know that his apartment will present challenges for home care. But no, she says, he won't be going anywhere. Palliative care in his case means stopping the transfusions that have been keeping him from dying until I arrived. The end will not be painful, she emphasizes. I tell her I plan to be staying across town and wonder about going there now and coming back in a few hours. *I'd stay here, if I were you*, she says. *It may not be long.* Only now do I surmise that the chaplain's aim in the meeting had been to help Bill say how he felt about dying.

By the time I return to Bill's room, an attendant has gotten him settled back into the bed. "Thirsty," Bill says, when I ask if he needs anything. I hold the cup of thickened juice to his lips. I have brought a picture of the two of us—me, a baby in a highchair looking down while laughing; Bill, a toddler with his head angled up, smiling into my eyes. I debate whether to take it out and show it to him. Decide not to. Bill, now more than ever, seems beyond sentimentality.

The resident in charge of Bill's case—the doctor I'd talked to on the phone—comes in. He goes to the opposite side of the bed from where I'm sitting and leans against the windowed wall, his hands behind his back. He looks young and awkward. His estimate about how long Bill will live is different from—longer than—the palliative care doctor's. He asks if I have questions. I shake my head. An hour after he leaves, a woman comes in and introduces herself as Bill's nephrologist, repeating the resident's performance. This must be part of the transition ritual, I think—decent people trying to provide a human touch. Bill sleeps through both visits.

I find I have an aversion to using the toilet in Bill's room. I step out to use the public bathroom down the hall and stop outside the room on the way back to call Katie. I'll be bunking with her for the rest of my stay. I see that a card has been put on the door with a quilt design printed on it. The signal, I guess, that the room's occupant was receiving only comfort measures. *Do you want me to come?* Katie asks. I tell her that only one person is allowed per day.

It occurs to me that I should call Pete, Robin or Rachel, and Joe. I don't have any of their phone numbers. I brought along a copy of the list of passwords that Bill had given me several years before. I try tapping several of the codes listed, one after another, on Bill's cell phone. None of them works. Bill wakes briefly. I ask him for his cell phone's code. He looks at me blankly, then turns his head away and dozes again.

When Bill's cell phone rings, I'm relieved to find I can answer it without a code. It's Joe. I explain who I am and the doctors' prediction that Bill will not live through the night. I find out that Joe has Bill's apartment keys, but not his car keys. Bill, Joe says, drove himself to the hospital, so those keys must be with him there. I ask him to give me numbers for Pete, and for Robin and Rachel. Bill wakes up while Joe and I are talking. I hold the phone to Bill's ear so he can hear Joe's voice. Bill seems to be listening. He nods a couple of times but doesn't say a word.

Bill's hand rests in mine as the hours unfold. I try to focus on his face, his breathing, holding him before God. My attention keeps wandering. I watch the numbers blink on the equipment next to the bed. I stare out the window, watching the yellow leaves of the courtyard trees let go one after the other and drift through the gray air to the pavers three floors below.

As I gaze into the murky courtyard, I think of how the wrathful souls in Dante's purgatory choke and squint through the smoke that was their earthly anger. At the bottom of Dante's hell there is an escape route, a narrow corkscrew turning toward purgatory's climb. A place in the afterlife set aside for purgation has no traction for me, but I know the bentness its chiropractic adjusts. A hummingbird lands briefly on a branch outside, then speeds away. It looks out of place, as if it has wandered into the wrong season.

Soon after that, someone knocks on the door. I open it and see a woman standing in the hallway carrying a small harp as if it were a grocery bag. The scarf draping the woman's neck displays brightly colored hummingbirds, larger than life. Campy, I think, especially in combination with the harp. (I am not making this up. If I've drifted into a dream, it is a dream in which improbabilities seem as real as the drone of the hallway exhaust fan and the blink of the monitors beside Bill's bed.)

She says she is a volunteer from the chaplain's office and will play for my brother, if he'd like. "Some people find it soothing," she says.

Bill, if he were still talking, would likely send her away, but I feel sorry for her. For fifteen minutes, she plays meandering melodies that I do not recognize. Bill shows no sign of being aware of her presence. She quietly leaves.

Returning to Bill's room after one of my trips down the hall, I find that someone has left a tray of fruit and small bags of cookies, chips, and crackers, as well as carafes of coffee and hot water for tea, along with cream, sugar, Splenda, and teabags. The note on the cellophane covering the food reads "Vigil Tray." I tear up for the first time that day. I've been subsisting on almonds and Kind bars from my purse. Someone has named what I am doing. Someone has thought of what I might need. The abundance of what they've provided throws me, as if those who know more than I do suspect this might go on indefinitely.

I eat an apple, savoring its crisp sweetness. I drink two cups of tea.

As the courtyard outside Bill's window darkens, my view through the windows across the hospital courtyard becomes startlingly clear. Two of the rooms look like lighted stage sets, making me wonder what Bill and I look like from across the way. Each of the rooms contains two people. In each room, one of the people wears PPE. The COVID wing, I guess.

In one of the rooms, a man sits on the bed, shirtless, while the backlit person in protective gear assists his sponge bath. The man's hair falls in heavy wet strands to his waist. After being left alone, he towels his hair, combs through it with his fingers, then flings his head with what looks like vanity but could be joy at being clean. I study the curve of his bare back, wondering if he is cold. The man retreats to the brightly lit room within his room. His posture indicates that he is on a toilet, though the toilet itself is hidden by the doorway's arch. I turn away.

I don't know how much longer I sat there before the warmth of life left the hand that I was holding. Neither Bill nor I had said aloud to one another that he was dying.

Simone Weil asserts that anyone "has his part in the Cross of Christ if he loves truth to the point of facing affliction rather than escape into the depths of falsehood." Weil believes that the cross is present in every affliction, even if concealed. The cross is available to anyone who chooses truth rather than falsehood and love rather than hate.

As Bill lay dying, I felt as if we were at the foot of the cross.

CHAPTER 16

Tin Lockbox

I used the intercom to let the hospital staff know that Bill was dead. It took a while for someone to come. The young man used his stethoscope, then called to ask for a second person, telling me that two people needed to verify a death. As the woman who'd made the verification left, the young man said, *We'll leave you alone now. Take as long as you like. Do you want us to send up someone from the chaplain's office?*

But I stood up and told him that I needed to go, that I was exhausted and still needed to drive myself across town to where I was staying. *Okay, but then you'll need to come back tomorrow to get your brother's things. They'll have them at the lobby desk. They'll also want to know about who will be coming for the body.*

I texted Katie to say I'd be there in half an hour. I would wait to call Steve until I got to her house. Before I left the hospital, I called Bill's friend, Joe, to let him know that Bill had died. We arranged a time to meet at Bill's apartment the next morning so he could give me Bill's keys.

The next morning Joe showed up at Bill's apartment house wearing khakis with crisp creases and a professionally ironed Oxford shirt. Slightly older than Bill, but lean and fit, he looked like someone on his way to a yacht club for brunch.

We went up the elevator separately, complying with the posted COVID instructions to use it one person at a time. On the door of Bill's apartment, the landlord had taped a flier about routes to follow out of the area if there were an evacuation because of wildfires.

The cleanness of Bill's apartment had cheered me when I first visited him here. Now the carpet was stained with spills and Willy's rebellion at being left alone too long. The kitchen counter overflowed with prescription bottles and unwashed dishes.

As we looked around, I asked if there was anything that Joe wanted to take. He walked over and picked up a cat platform whose scratching posts showed that Little Willy had been putting them to use. "Okay if I take this?" he asked.

"Of course," I responded. "Anything else?"

Joe scanned the living room and shook his head. "Maybe Pete would want the computer. He put in a lot of time helping Bill with debugging."

Joe's lack of interest in my brother's things shamed me. That and the contrast between how he was dressed and the jeans I was wearing. Whether or not Joe saw himself above Bill and me, I felt looked down upon.

"There's something I want to ask you if you don't mind," Joe said, as he looked directly into my eyes. "I never asked Bill, but I hope he knew Jesus as his Lord and Savior."

I hesitated before responding, wondering what the point of this kind, nosy stranger asking me this now might be. "He was baptized when he was nine, Joe. Jesus knew him. God loves him." I sensed that Joe found my response inadequate. He left soon after that, carrying the cat platform and saying to let him know if he could be of other help.

I opened drawers in the small desk, pulling out Bill's checkbook, documents from his last bankruptcy filing, other papers that might give clues to Bill's current debtors, an old address book. In his bedroom closet, I found a tin document box with a combination lock.

I was relieved to find it wasn't locked and that it contained the deed for the cemetery plot Bill would share with our parents. Next to it was a bronze plaque attesting that Bill Miller was certified for excellence as an auto mechanic by the National Institute for Automotive Service Excellence. Along with these, I found a postcard I had written to him while on a trip to Scotland ten years earlier. A castle in a Highland glen. I had no memory of having written its forgettable message. There was also a pocket watch, its yellowed crystal cracked. Why had Bill kept it? I found no will or notes about final intentions.

I put the items from the desk into the tin box. From a shelf of the curio cabinet next to the desk, I added a framed 4 x 6 snapshot of the two of us at a party a decade earlier. I was surprised to see it was sitting beside a photo of Elenore with her daughter, Ashley. Bill and Elenore's breakup had not been pretty. They'd been together for quite a few years, often quarreling, but also supporting one another through challenges, including Elenore's treatment for breast cancer. Odd that the last straw for Elenore had been something relatively minor: Bill's lack of interest in helping to decorate for Ashley's sixteenth birthday party. I wondered if I should call her. I wondered whether the number in the address book would still be good.

Before leaving, I scanned the rooms. From Bill's small bookshelf, I took a leather-bound *Pictorial History of American Sports*, its corners soft with wear. I thought I remembered it from our childhood. It and the contents of the tin box could fit in my carry-on for the return flight. I planned to come back in a day or two to box up the few things worth keeping: an almost new Instant Pot that Katie might want, a dozen pool and racquetball trophies from Bill's glory days, two truck-shaped toy savings banks with Texaco emblems painted on their sides that I could give to my granddaughters. I could ask Steve's brother, John, if he wanted the TV. I wondered whether there was some service that I could hire to empty the apartment and give away what was worth giving, trashing the rest.

I drove back to the hospital. I went to the reception desk, explaining why I was there. The woman went away and came back with what looked like a white garbage bag containing personal items including the clothes Bill had had with him when he checked in. Was there something I needed to sign? She shook her head. I told her I would call tomorrow about who would be coming for Bill's body.

Back in my rented car, I trolled the parking garage, then the surface lots, looking for Bill's white Malibu. I'd fished its key out of the bag containing Bill's things. I finally found it parked in a handicapped space in the lot nearest the emergency entrance. I felt stupid for not starting my search there. I rolled down my window and clicked the button on the Malibu's key fob to verify it was the right car. The taillights blinked. I drove away without getting out of my car. I planned to return with Katie, thinking that she could drive Bill's car to her place and keep it there for the time being.

When I got back to Katie's house, I found a lawyer's phone number in Bill's address book. Calling, I was told that, though they had handled a bankruptcy filing for Bill, they knew nothing about a will. No one at their firm handled estate law.

The next morning, I met with two women at Sunset Hills cemetery. We sat at opposite ends of a long conference table, as they explained apologetically that, because of COVID, the soonest date for Bill's cremation would be in three weeks. I said that I would not be in town that long. They asked if there was anyone else who'd want to be present at the cremation. I said no, but that I was inviting people to an informal graveside service on Saturday, if that was permitted. They offered catering—boxed lunches—which I declined. I had no idea how many people would be there; I'd asked Robin, Rachel, Pete, and Joe to spread the word among people who'd known Bill about what time we were meeting.

One of the women explained options for a cremation urn. The other handed me a catalog of grave markers, saying decisions about that could be made later. Something so simple had taken an hour and a half, mainly because of the long wait between the time that one of them stepped out of the room to process my credit card and returned with two copies of the contract for me to sign. Head nods took the place of handshakes as they showed me out of the room.

Afterwards, feeling in desperate need of a long walk, I drove the two miles to Washington Park. As I got to the entrance of one of its parking lots, I saw that the gate was down and there was a large sign saying that the park was closed. No explanation. COVID? Fire risk? Both were equally likely.

I drove on through the smog-cloaked streets, thinking that I was snaking back toward Katie's house, but instead found myself in the trendy Goose Hollow neighborhood on the eastern slope of Portland's West Hills. I saw that homeless people had set up small tents on the parking strips in front of closed storefronts. I wondered when the city's slogan *Keeping Portland Weird* had been replaced by *Abandon Hope All Ye Who Enter Here.*

I drove to a suburban outdoor mall near Katie's and walked laps around the mostly empty parking lot in front of Best Buy, Target, and T. J. Maxx for an hour. The place looked scarcely more hopeful than the homeless encampments. Returning to Katie's house, I stretched out on the guest-room bed and tried to read an Agatha Christie novel, *The Mirror Crack'd from Side to Side* which I'd begun reading on my Kindle during the flight to Portland.

Later that day, Katie mentioned that she knew someone who was an estate attorney. I called his office and explained my situation to the assistant who answered the phone. She said that she could set up an appointment with the lawyer for me, but that the minimum for handling a petition to be appointed executor of my brother's estate would be $900. Without such a filing, my legal standing would be nil. Until his estate was settled, whether I was appointed executor or not, I would have no right to sell any of his things or give them away. Legally, I could put his stuff in storage if I chose, but I had no obligation to do anything. If I left things as they were, the state would conduct the probate process.

I had asked Bill more than once during the week before I flew out, "Is there anything you want me to know? Is there anything you want me to do for you?" meaning *Do you want me to come? Do you want to tell me you are dying? Anything you want me to do with your stuff if you die?* His answer had always been, "No. No. Nothing."

I pondered whether to wade into months of cross-continent complications or walk away. Mentally, I guessed at the cash value of the contents of Bill's apartment, plus the car and his unknown bank balance. I subtracted the unknown amount of his outstanding debts and the costs of the lawyer and a storage unit. I called Steve to see what he thought. *Whatever you decide*, he said.

My time in Portland had made me feel like a COVID refugee, every small errand fraught with risk. Probate would take months. Much of what needed to be done could not be done at a distance. I would need to stay on or make a trip back. My husband and new home full of boxes still to be unpacked were waiting for me on the other side of the country.

The next day, I put the key to Bill's apartment in an envelope with a typed, unsigned note stating that William Miller was deceased and addressed it to his apartment building's manager. I left the upper left-hand corner of the envelope blank. As I dropped it in the mail slot, I felt like someone fleeing the scene of an accident.

I never went back to get Bill's car. I hoped, with little confidence, that when it was impounded, the proceeds from the sale would compensate the hospital for the bills that would go unpaid.

"Only perfection is sufficient." So Simone Weil writes in a letter dated May 26, 1942. The letter, which the editor of *Waiting for God* entitled "Last Thoughts," was to a priest who'd become her friend. Weil died a little over a year later. Her belief that only perfection is sufficient explains much about her life. She pushed herself relentlessly. She saw affliction as preferrable to mediocrity.

"My grace is sufficient for you, for power is made perfect in weakness," the apostle Paul reports that God told him.

Whom do you side with, Weil or Paul? Both saw perfection and grace as two sides of the same coin. Still, it matters which side of the coin you focus on. For Bill's sake, and for my own, I side with Paul.

The Saturday after Bill's death, a handful of his friends gathered with Katie, John, and me around the grave that Bill would share with our parents. It had rained the day before and, for the first time since I'd landed in Portland, the air was clear. For once, I was grateful for COVID, which could explain the dearth of mourners and absence of pomp. Rachel, Robin, Pete, and a few others were there. Joe was not. Nor was Elenore, who I had not tried to call but thought might have gotten word through others.

The dampness of the ground penetrated my shoes as I read a page of prepared remarks. I talked about Bill's love of fixing things, his work ethic, and his contradictions: fierce independence coupled with demandingness; his love of socializing over dinners and drinks combined with being tight-lipped about his feelings. I also talked about his sense of adventure, love of competition, and the times he had gone out of his way to care for other people. My reference to Matthew 25, where Christ separates the sheep from the goats and all are surprised at who are welcomed into his kingdom, was aimed mainly at Bill's absent friend Joe.

I asked whether others had memories they wanted to share. After an awkward pause, Rachel and Pete each shared a story about Bill—how much fun he'd been on road trips, how he'd made them laugh. I invited people to take a beer or a Coke from the cooler I'd brought and drink it in memory of Bill. A man who I had not met came up afterward and said his name was Bucky. He explained that he'd taken trips with Bill, Robin, and Rachel, including a memorable one to Las Vegas. He caught Robin's eye, and they laughed together over some memory they could jointly savor without describing it.

After the others left, I continued to talk with Robin and Rachel, who told me about yet another of their cross-country Harley trips with Bill. I commented to them on how calm Bill had been in his last hours. Rachel looked me in the eye and said, "He was very afraid of dying."

Epilogue

After leaving the cemetery, I drove toward an airport hotel, having used the excuse of an early morning flight to avoid staying another night at Katie's. I wanted to be alone.

When I saw the Halsey Street exit off the Banfield freeway, I took it, pulling into the first parking lot I came to. Though my family had taken that exit a thousand times when I was a child, I no longer knew my way. I put the address of the Sacramento Street house where Bill and I had lived during grade school into my maps program.

A short while later, I pulled to the curb and sat looking through the windshield at the house's light gray exterior. How many colors had it been through in the five decades since it had been the faded brick red I remembered? The lawn was weedless. The carport had been converted into a single-stall garage. The partial fence that had supported climbing roses and hidden the bedroom windows from passersby was gone. Though well kept, the house looked tiny, dreary, and exposed.

After checking into the hotel, I stretched out on the bed and tried to read. As dinnertime neared, I went to the small convenience center next to the front desk and bought a half bottle of white wine, taking it back to the room and putting it in the bucket half full of ice. I remembered passing a McDonald's just a block away, so I walked in that direction. When I got there, I realized that, because of COVID, only its drive-through window was open, so I walked back to get the car. Returning, I ordered a double cheeseburger without a bun and a vanilla shake.

I hadn't had a McDonald's shake in years. With the wine, having one now made little sense. But after eating the burger, I drank part of the shake, remembering the one I'd fed a spoonful at a time to Bill six years earlier. I emptied the rest of it into the bathroom sink and ran the tap until it all went down the drain. Feeling both overfull and hollow, I watched *Law & Order* reruns while sipping the wine. I woke up to an infomercial about reverse mortgages. Looking at the clock, I saw that it was 3 a.m. My alarm was set for 4:30.

I got up and showered and headed to the rental car return. My flight didn't leave until 8, but I could walk laps on the concourse after going through TSA.

Which brings us back to where this book began, with me disembarking from my return flight, wrung out but restless, at odds with myself, undone. Angrier than I could remember ever having been. What do you make of that anger?

Being thwarted had something to do with it. I had thought myself so smart, so able to get things done. Simone Weil says this about pride in one's intelligence: "The difference between people more or less intelligent is like the difference between prisoners condemned to life in prison whose cells are more or less large. An intelligent man who is proud of his intelligence is like a prisoner who is proud of having a big cell." The week my brother died had rubbed my nose in that reality.

A visceral reaction to affliction was a larger part of it. To clearly see the afflicted is not only to agonize with them, but to see that nothing protects you from becoming like them. Flying home from Portland, I knew in my gut—in my bones—that there was nothing the play of circumstances could not snatch from me at any time. My lack of anger during those bouts of feeling on the verge of death in 2018 was, I now think, rooted in my confidence that what I'd worked for all my life would go on mattering. My life would have an afterlife, not just in eternity, but in the here and now. In September 2020, I was grieving not just my brother's death, but that he'd died with so little of what he'd worked for and cared about intact. Concurrently, a pandemic, natural disasters, man-made and otherwise, and a looming presidential election the outcome of which might put the United States on an irreversible authoritarian path made me wonder how long anything most of us had worked for would endure.

The pandemic taught many of us, in diverse ways, the lesson that whole ways of life could be disrupted with little warning. Many of us swiftly forgot. As I write, it's been four years since COVID vaccines began restoring a modicum of normality to our lives. Since then, reality, in the form of larger, more frequent wildfires, more extreme weather events, and more profound political disruptions, looks hell-bent on keeping the fragility of what we cherish at the forefront of our minds. What circumstances will be the undoing of each of us varies, because what matters most to each of us varies, as does how—long after our death—each of us wants our lives to go on mattering.

When I describe myself as "undone" after my brother's death, I am, of course, exaggerating. Foreboding of affliction is not itself affliction, nor is vicarious participation in it. Caregivers can be undone by caregiving—physically, emotionally, and spiritually spent, impoverished, and bereft of their former social identity. I was not one of them. I was grieving and socially disoriented, but physically I was fine. Suffering but not afflicted.

Simone Weil thought that, ultimately, those who are fully in touch with reality welcome affliction as a precious gift, as the beauty of the world penetrating a human body. Out of love for the God who made the world, we should be able to consent to all that is in it, including affliction for ourselves and for those we love. My anger was my sharp dissent, and my dissent was not just self-referential. My brother, having survived his 2013 cardiopulmonary crisis, had wanted himself back before he died. I found no beauty in life's denying him that. I found that an outrage.

I hear Weil saying to me: *You've yet to learn how to read God's ways with requisite wisdom.* Fair enough. But my faith is less stoic than Weil's. She and I both follow a Christ who was obedient unto death, even death on the cross. But my Lord also wept over Lazareth's death. Though he affirmed that it had happened for God's glory, Jesus showed no sign of finding beauty in the stench produced by his friend's entombment.

I arranged for the cemetery to install a marker on Bill's grave etched with a Harley-Davidson alongside his name and dates, hoping he would have thought it fitting. I was under no illusion that it made up for my distant presence, my imperfect attention, my leaving his affairs in disarray.

My brother's apartment manager called me a few weeks after Bill died. He said I was listed as Bill's emergency contact and asked if I planned to clear out his apartment. I told him what the attorney that I'd talked to had said: that I had no legal rights or obligations regarding my brother's things. The man said I'd be receiving a form to sign and return, stating that the contents of the apartment were worth less than a thousand dollars and that I understood that meant he had a right to dispose of them. I told him that I thought that the contents of Bill's apartment were worth more than a thousand dollars and that I did not know what he had a right to do with them. I would not sign his form. He said he'd mail it anyway.

I sent my oldest son, Paul, the pocket watch with the cracked crystal that I found among Bill's things. Paul's middle name is Wesley, after my father. I choose to believe the watch belonged to Paul's great-grandfather, William Miller—that my father had kept it and passed it on to Bill. Maybe my son will keep the watch in memory of his grandfather and great-grandfather, who died years before he was born. I will not ask. I am a Miller, after all.

I have pondered many questions in doing my long, slow postmortem of what kind of sister I'd been to Bill Miller. I have often wondered how Rachel was so sure of Bill's fear of dying. Was Bill willing to express his fears to a woman who was not his little sister? Or did it have something to do with what Simone Weil says about how talent, energy, character, and strong personality often function as self-protective screens preventing genuine connection with the afflicted? To help the afflicted, she says, "It is not necessary to go after the screen, but it is necessary to put it carefully to the side, while trying to make sure that as little as possible is seen of it." Had Rachel been able to put aside those barriers between the afflicted and those who are trying to help in a way that I could not? In any case, I am glad that Bill had such a friend.

Weil observes that, because those who are afflicted know they are not being heard, they become impotent in using language. They may keep talking, but their words are empty. How often had my failures to listen well enough kept Bill from saying what he needed most to say? Often enough to make me writhe in hindsight.

Simone Weil tells us that "Listening to someone is to put ourselves in his place while he is speaking." Weil thought that people seldom really listen to the afflicted in no small part because we do not want to put ourselves in their place. Real listening requires the kind of attention that opens us to another without trying to fit him into a category. My brother and I talked more during the last six years of his life than in the prior four decades combined. Too often I was listening only through a scrim of categories: inconsiderate, alcoholic, closed-mouthed, tough, needy, noncompliant dialysis patient. And brother—brother too is, after all, a category.

Weil also observes that the same set of circumstances may plunge one person into affliction but not another. She also says that the line between suffering and affliction is like the boiling point of water. When did my brother's slide toward affliction begin? Was it when his business failed or when his last boss took away his benefits and tried to hound him into quitting? And when did Bill cross the line between "mere" suffering and actual affliction: when he became a dialysis patient, or when he was removed from the kidney transplant list, or when his sister met his remark about moving in with her with silence? Questions that God alone can answer. Questions that when asked by one human being of another reduce affliction to just another category.

The point of pondering affliction is not so that we can accurately sort humanity into two camps: the afflicted and those who are not. Instead, becoming sensitive to the possibility of affliction makes us treat each human being we encounter—especially those we find least prepossessing—as having a depth beyond our ken. As a mystery, not to be solved, but to be saluted.

For a long time, I wondered about questions only Bill could have answered. Had he thought when he drove himself to the hospital that he might die there? Had he left a note on the passenger seat of the Malibu that I would have found if I'd at least looked inside before I'd driven away?

I have also wondered about the postcard from me that I found in Bill's apartment. Why had he kept it? Why had he put it in that document box with the deed to the cemetery plot? At the bottom of that list of passwords Bill had given me in 2014, after the lot number for our parents' burial plot and "Cremation okay," and before "My bucket list—a motorcycle trip to see the country at my leisure," he'd written "If this cemetery plot has resale value, spread my ashes on your travels." Had Bill pictured me scattering his ashes on the Isle of Skye?

What I didn't find in the apartment also intrigues me. Not finding a will was inconvenient but unsurprising. But what had become of the picture of the bare-breasted Vegas show girls that had been in his desk six years before? Had Bill cleared out what he had not wanted me or some friend to see? Perhaps he performed his own version of putting his affairs in order.

Simone Weil observes that those who exhibit true Christian love for the afflicted meet their needs as instinctively as one feeds oneself when hungry. How often did I meet Bill's needs in that way? That's a question I can answer. The answer is: Not often enough.

I did not prevent, nor perhaps even appreciably lessen, Bill Miller's suffering, but I have at least borne witness to it. Attention must be paid to such a person. Attention is love's main ingredient.

Acknowledgments

My cherished friends Lynne M. Baab, Ann Baker, Christopher C. Barney, Garret Keizer, and Patricia O'Connell Killen generously used their time to read and comment on earlier versions of this book. Their insights about form and substance were invaluable.

My husband, Stephen C. Simon, proofread an embarrassingly high number of iterations of the manuscript, saving me from having to parade my dyslexia before others. Steve's supportiveness and practical help as I weathered the vicissitudes retold in this book are less visible in this telling than they were in the living. My life would be unimaginably diminished without all the decades of love we've shared.

I wrote much of this book while participating in writing communities facilitated by Sarah Sentilles. The atmosphere of creative energy and mutual encouragement in those Word Rivers and Word Caves breathed hope into me when I needed it most.

Laura Gifford and her editorial team at Fortress Press asked great questions that significantly improved the clarity and structure of the book. They have been a joy to work with.

Portions of Chapters 7 and 10, in modified form, appeared as the essay "Dorothy Day Might Have Liked My Brother" in *The Other Journal* 38 (Fall 2024).

Why Simone Weil?

Readers who have never heard of Simone Weil may well wonder why I'm paying so much attention to her in this book. The simple answer is that I know of no one who has provided more insight into the complex form of suffering that she calls affliction. I also find Weil's purity of heart compelling. By purity of heart, I don't mean that she was without faults. She was eccentric, demanding, and lacking in social grace. Yet she had a passionate desire to seek truth and shape her life by the truths she thought she'd found.

Simone Weil's search brought her to love Christ crucified and to embrace Christ's command to love our neighbor, especially the poor and outcast. Christ's command to love, she thought, entailed more than sentimental feeling; it meant costly action. The Danish philosopher Søren Kierkegaard sneers at philosophers who build palaces of thought but live in a dog kennel beside their palace, never bothering to practice what their philosophy demands. Simone Weil pitched a tent in the construction zone of her philosophy, living her way into envisioning its vaulted ceilings and upper floors. Though the palace of her thought remained incomplete when she died at age thirty-four, thousands of articles and books have been written about her.

Here, in brief, is a sketch of Simone Weil's life. She was born in Paris on February 3, 1909, to wealthy parents who were ethnic Jews but free thinkers, shaped by the post-Christian intellectual culture of late nineteenth-century and early twentieth-century France. She remained close to her older brother, André, her whole life. André's foundational work in number theory and algebraic geometry made him one of the most influential mathematicians of the twentieth century.

In 1931, Simone was one of the first women to graduate from the prestigious École Normale Supérieure. Though she suffered from frequent migraine headaches over the whole of her adult life, she threw herself headfirst into living. She taught in a lycée (part of what we would call the K-12 system) for several years after graduating, while also teaching classes for workers in her free time. In 1934 and 1935, she worked in three different factories in order to directly share the experience of industrial labor. In 1936, she went to fight for the Republicans in the Spanish Civil War. When the Germans invaded France in 1940, her family left Paris and lived in Marseille until 1942. There she worked for the French Resistance distributing literature while also working on a fishing boat and, later, doing agricultural labor in grape fields. During this time, she also wrote much of the material that would be published after her death.

In the 1930s, Weil had at least three vivid personal religious experiences involving Christ. These helped her grasp how love, "like the smile on a beloved face," could be present even in the midst of affliction. While in Marseille, she had extensive religious discussions with Father Jean-Marie Perrin, a Catholic priest. She believed in the Trinity, and the incarnation, crucifixion, and resurrection of Christ. She practiced fervent private devotion and frequently participated in Christian worship services. Perrin hoped that she would be baptized, but she thought that her vocation involved loving God from outside official membership in the institutional church.

In June 1942, Weil left France with her parents for New York. There, she tried to convince the US military to parachute her behind enemy lines so that she could lead a group of nurses in delivering care to the wounded on all sides of the conflict. When those efforts were unsuccessful, she left New York for London in November 1942. There she worked for the Free French, writing reports on what would need to happen to rebuild French cultural and civic structures once the Germans were expelled from France. After her death, those materials were gathered into her book, *The Need for Roots: Prelude to a Declaration of Duties Towards Mankind*. From April 1943 to her death on August 24, 1943, she was hospitalized with tuberculosis. She kept her illness a secret from her parents and brother, who were still living in the United States at the time.

After her death, Weil's parents and friends transcribed many of her notebooks. This material, along with her letters, was subsequently edited for publication, the best-known compilation being her book *Waiting for God*. Gustave Thibon, a friend she had made while living in Marseille, organized some of the notebook material she'd left with him topically and published it as *Gravity and Grace*. Her views on the nature and theological import of affliction have been pondered by thinkers as diverse as poet T. S. Eliot, atheistic novelist and philosopher Albert Camus, psychologist and writer Robert Coles, and Christian philosophical theologian Diogenes Allen.

Notes

AUTHOR'S NOTE

xii ***gripping novel,* Affliction, *became the basis for a compelling movie:*** Russell Banks, *Affliction* (Harper & Row, 1989). The film *Affliction*, released in 1997, was written and directed by Paul Schrader, with major roles played by Nick Nolte, Sissy Spacek, James Coburn, and Willem Dafoe.

xii ***"an accident can at any time wipe out what I am":*** Simone Weil, "What Is Sacred in Every Human Being?," *Late Philosophical Writings*, ed. Eric O. Springsted, trans. Eric O. Springsted and Lawrence E. Schmidt (Notre Dame University Press, 2015), 122.

xii ***Only those heroically devoted to truth refrain from fictionalizing their pasts:*** Simone Weil, "Morality and Literature," *On Science, Necessity and the Love of God*, ed. and trans. Richard Rees (Oxford University Press, 1968), 161.

INTRODUCTION

2 ***Simone Weil calls it "the great enigma of human life":*** Simone Weil, "The Love of God and Affliction," *Waiting for God*, ed. and trans. Emma Craufurd (first published in 1951 by G. P. Putnam's Sons; reprint, Harper Perennial, 2009), 68.

2 ***distinguishes it from pain, suffering, and sorrow:*** Simone Weil, "The Love of God and Affliction," *Waiting for God*, 68.

2 ***hiddenness of affliction is that it renders the afflicted inarticulate:*** Simone Weil, "The Love of God and Affliction," *Waiting for God*, 69.

3 ***each of us is involved at least in the guilt of criminal indifference:*** Simone Weil, "The Love of God and Affliction," *On Science, Necessity and the Love of God*, ed. and trans. Richard Rees (Oxford University Press, 1968), 184. NB: There are two different versions of this essay. The version in *On Science, Necessity and the Love of God* is less easily accessed but contains material not in *Waiting for God*.

3 ***Weil says it always entails self-loss:*** Simone Weil, "Forms of Implicit Love of God," *Waiting for God*, 92.

3 ***to witness from "the intersection of Christianity and everything that is not:*** Simone Weil, "Letter IV: Spiritual Autobiography," *Waiting for God*, 32.

CHAPTER 1: CAREENING DOWNHILL

11 ***French workmen say, "It's the trade getting into his body:*** Simone Weil, "The Love of God and Affliction," *Waiting for God*, 78.

11 ***held that physical labor is not in itself degrading:*** Simone Weil, "What Is Sacred in Every Human Being?," *Late Philosophical Writings*, 112.

11 ***skilled manual labor and was contrasted with the professions:*** *Oxford English Dictionary*, "trade (n.)," March 2025, https://doi.org/10.1093/OED/6330135678.

11 ***robs manual labor of its dignity:*** Francine de Plessix Gray, *Simone Weil* (Viking Penguin, 2001), 90, 101–102.

CHAPTER 3: HOLEY SAFETY NET

19 ***the most tortuous job requirement was deference to arbitrary authority:*** Francine de Plessix Gray, *Simone Weil*, 98.

CHAPTER 4: UNDER THE RUBBLE

27 ***Simone Weil admired Charlie Chaplin's Modern Times:*** Francine de Plessix Gray, *Simone Weil*, 88.

27 ***pulled into the cogs of a machine. He is nothing more than a torn and bloodied thing":*** Simone Weil, "What is Sacred in Every Human Being?," *Late Philosophical Writings*, 121.

27 ***All affliction involves social degradation, or the fear of it:*** Simone Weil, "The Love of God and Affliction," *Waiting for God*, 68.

28 ***affliction sneaks up on its victims:*** Simone Weil, "The Love of God and Affliction," *Waiting for God*, 68.

28 ***To live is to be slowly born:*** Antoine de Saint-Exupéry, *Flight to Arras*, trans. Lewis Galantière (Harcourt Brace, 1942), 41.

CHAPTER 5: MORE THAN CAUTIONARY TALES

42 ***anxious over whether she'd sleep well enough to survive the next day's work:*** Francine de Plessix Gray, *Simone Weil*, 38, 39–41, 92.

CHAPTER 6: NOT SEEING THE WHOLE CHESSBOARD

49 ***when two beings who are not friends are near each other there is no meeting:*** Simone Weil, "The Love of God and Affliction," *Waiting for God*, 74.

49 ***This love, this friendship of God, is the Trinity:*** Simone Weil, "The Love of God and Affliction," *Waiting for God*, 74.

50 ***Christ's self-emptying, which is at the same time the creation, the incarnation, and the crucifixion:*** Lissa McCullough, *The Religious Philosophy of Simone Weil: An Introduction* (I.B. Tauris, 2014), 238.

50 ***affliction being transformed into ultimate good through participation in Christ's cross:*** Eric O. Springsted, *Simone Weil for the Twenty-First Century* (Notre Dame University Press, 2021), 43.

CHAPTER 7: DOROTHY DAY NEVER KNEW MY BROTHER

51 ***followers of Christ have no right to discriminate between the deserving and undeserving poor:*** Dorothy Day, "Catholic Worker Ideas of Hospitality," *The Catholic Worker* (May 1940), 10.

53 ***should know about the poor. They tend to smell, and they are ungrateful:*** Robert Barron, *Bridging the Great Divide* (Sheed & Ward, 2004), 29.

59 ***In just the same way God looks after each soul as if it had no equal:*** Saint Thérèse of Lisieux, *The Autobiography of Saint Thérèse of Lisieux*, trans. John Beevers (Doubleday, 1957), 20.

60 ***"Fraternity is the creation of sacrifices alone,":*** Antoine de Saint-Exupéry, *Flight to Arras*, 148.

60 ***"To create love, we must begin by sacrifice.":*** Antoine de Saint-Exupéry, *Flight to Arras*, 150.

60 ***something repulsive ("a half-crushed worm writhing on the ground"), compassion for the afflicted is a miracle:*** Simone Weil, "The Love of God and Affliction," *Waiting for God*, 69.

CHAPTER 8: STUNG

64 ***"yin-yang children who shaped and were shaped by each other.":*** Karen Olsson, *The Weil Conjecture: On Math and the Pursuit of the Unknown* (Farrar, Straus and Giroux, 2019), 64.

68 ***circumstances may plunge one person into affliction but not another:*** Simone Weil, "The Love of God and Affliction," *Waiting for God*, 69.

68 ***injects inertia into the soul, making the afflicted person complicit in his own affliction:*** Simone Weil, "The Love of God and Affliction," *Waiting for God*, 71.

68 ***affliction had established itself in him like a parasite:*** Simone Weil, "The Love of God and Affliction," *Waiting for God*, 72.

CHAPTER 9: HEAD OF THE HOUSE

74 ***folds imposed upon the waves by gravity. That is why they contain an element of beauty:*** Simone Weil, "The Love of God and Affliction," *Waiting for God*, 76.

74 ***Gerard Manley Hopkins memorializes five nuns who died in a shipwreck:*** Gerard Manley Hopkins, "The Wreck of the Deutschland," *The Major Works*, ed. Catherine Phillips (Oxford University Press, 2002), 110–119.

75 ***with Julian of Norwich, that God* will *make all things well:*** Julian of Norwich, *Showings*, trans. Edmund College, O.S.A., and James Walsh, S.J. (Paulist Press, 1978), 151.

CHAPTER 10: STRETCHING OUT A WITHERED LIMB

83 ***had no stomach for trying to barter my kidney for my brother's sobriety:*** Simone Weil does not find it surprising that those who have a surplus give some of it to those in dire need. What is surprising, she says, is for someone to be "capable of doing so with so different a gesture from that with which we buy an object. Almsgiving when it is not supernatural is like a sort of purchase. It buys the sufferer." Simone Weil, "Forms of Implicit Love of God," *Waiting for God*, 91.

84 ***"To live is to be slowly born.":*** Antoine de Saint-Exupéry, *Flight to Arras*, 41.

CHAPTER 11: BOUTS OF FRAGILITY

89 ***She reminds us that cherry blossoms are more beautiful for being frail.:*** Simone Weil, "The Love of God and Affliction," *On Science, Necessity and the Love of God*, 185.

89 ***Emily Dickinson's "formal feeling," which she said comes after pain:*** Emily Dickinson, "After great pain, a formal feeling comes," poem 341 in *The Complete Poems of Emily Dickinson*, ed. Thomas H. Johnson (Little, Brown, 1960).

CHAPTER 12: PULLING AWAY

96 ***as anyone does when they see death in its nakedness, not dressed up:*** Simone Weil, "What Is Sacred in Every Human Being?," *Late Philosophical Writings*, 122.

96 ***Weil reminds us that "Why?" has two meanings:*** "By what cause?" and "For what purpose?": Simone Weil, "The Love of God and Affliction," *Waiting for God*, 196.

97 ***sacred in every human heart is the expectation that good and not evil will be done to us.:*** Simone Weil, "What Is Sacred in Every Human Being?," *Late Philosophical Writings*, 105.

97 ***"become impotent in using language because of the certitude that they are not heard.":*** Simone Weil, "What Is Sacred in Every Human Being?," *Late Philosophical Writings*, 122.

97 ***sacred part of the afflicted is not dead, but mute:*** Simone Weil, "What Is Sacred in Every Human Being?," *Late Philosophical Writings*, 106.

97 ***It fosters a sense of guilt and defilement:*** Simone Weil, "The Love of God and Affliction," *Waiting for God*, 70–71.

CHAPTER 13: SMELLS OF CHILDHOOD

102 ***". . .vast, unmeasured, boundless, free. . ." looping through my mind:*** Samuel Trevor Francis, "Oh, the Deep, Deep Love of Jesus" (written 1875), Hymn 796 in *Lift Up Your Heart: Psalms, Hymns, and Spiritual Songs* (Faith Alive, 2013).

CHAPTER 14: DUSTY GUEST ROOM

106 ***tactless sympathy will make the afflicted person feel like a specimen:*** Simone Weil, "The Love of God and Affliction," *On Science, Necessity and the Love of God*, 189.

106 ***tries either by lying or unconsciousness to make himself deaf to himself:*** Simone Weil, "What Is Sacred in Every Human Being?," *Late Philosophical Writings*, 122–23.

107 ***preserve their self-respect that Weil claims that this only happens supernaturally:*** Simone Weil, "Forms of Implicit Love of God," *Waiting for God*, 91.

109 ***famous on Silko's Laguna reservation solely for the fact of being alive:*** Leslie Marmon Silko and James Wright, *The Delicacy and Strength of Lace*, ed. Anne Wright (Graywolf Press, 1986), 98–99.

CHAPTER 15: VIGIL

113 ***impenitent thief if we seek consolation in contempt:*** Simone Weil, "The Love of God and Affliction," *On Science, Necessity and the Love of God*, 182, 183.

113 ***give to the afflicted, but only through the supernatural operation of grace:*** Simone Weil, "What Is Sacred in Every Human Being?," *Late Philosophical Writings*, 123.

113 ***present at the point where the eyes of those who give and those who receive meet:*** Simone Weil, "Forms of Implicit Love of God," *Waiting for God*, 93–94.

118 ***part in the Cross of Christ if he loves truth to the point of facing affliction:*** Simone Weil, "The Love of God and Affliction," *On Science, Necessity and the Love of God*, 194.

CHAPTER 16: TIN LOCKBOX

124 ***"Only perfection is sufficient":*** Simone Weil, "Letter VI: Last Thoughts," *Waiting for God*, 48.

124 ***saw affliction as preferrable to mediocrity:*** Simone Weil, "The Love of God and Affliction," *On Science, Necessity and the Love of God*, 198.

124 ***power is made perfect in weakness:*** Corinthians 12:9 NRSVUE.

EPILOGUE

128 ***proud of his intelligence is like a prisoner who is proud of having a big cell:*** Simone Weil, "What Is Sacred in Every Human Being?," *Late Philosophical Writings*, 120.

128 ***but to see that nothing protects you from becoming like them:*** Simone Weil, "What Is Sacred in Every Human Being?," *Late Philosophical Writings*, 122.

129 ***consent to all that is in it, including affliction for ourselves and for those we love:*** Simone Weil, "The Love of God and Affliction," *Waiting for God*, 78.

129 ***But my faith is less stoic than Weil's:*** Simone Weil, "Letter VI: Last Thoughts," *Waiting for God*, 48–49.

131 ***not necessary to go after the screen, but it is necessary to put it carefully to the side:*** Simone Weil, "What Is Sacred in Every Human Being?," *Late Philosophical Writings*, 119.

131 ***they become impotent in using language:*** Simone Weil, "What Is Sacred in Every Human Being?," *Late Philosophical Writings*, 122.

131 ***put ourselves in his place while he is speaking:*** Simone Weil, "What Is Sacred in Every Human Being?," *Late Philosophical Writings*, 122.

131 ***attention that opens us to another without trying to fit him into a category:*** Eric O. Springsted, *Simone Weil for the Twenty-First Century*, 56.

132 ***meet their needs as instinctively as one feeds oneself when hungry:*** Simone Weil, "The Love of God and Affliction," *On Science, Necessity and the Love of God*, 190.

132 ***Attention is love's main ingredient:*** Simone Weil, "Forms of Implicit Love of God," *Waiting for God*, 92.

WHY SIMONE WEIL?

136 ***helped her grasp how love, "like the smile on a beloved face":*** Simone Weil, "Letter IV: Spiritual Autobiography," *Waiting for God*, 27.

Recommended Reading

SIMONE WEIL'S WRITINGS ON AFFLICTION:

Simone Weil, *Waiting for God*, ed. and trans Emma Craufurd (first published in 1951 by G. P. Putnam's Sons; reprint, Harper Perennial, 2009), especially "The Love of God and Affliction" and "Forms of Implicit Love of God."

Simone Weil, "What Is Sacred in Every Human Being?," *Late Philosophical Writings*, ed. Eric O. Springsted, trans. Eric O. Springsted and Lawrence E. Schmidt (Notre Dame University Press, 2015).

DISCUSSION OF SIMONE WEIL'S VIEWS ON AFFLICTION:

Lissa McCullough, *The Religious Philosophy of Simone Weil: An Introduction* (I.B. Tauris, 2014).

Insese Radzins, "Affliction and the Option for the Poor," in *The Relevance of the Radical: Simone Weil 100 Years Later*, eds. Rebecca Rozelle-Stone and Lucian Stone (Continuum, 2010).

Eric O. Springsted, *Simone Weil for the Twenty-First Century* (Notre Dame University Press, 2021).

Robert Zaretsky, *The Subversive Simone Weil: A Life in Five Ideas* (University of Chicago Press, 2021), especially Chapter One, "The Force of Affliction." This book straddles this category and the next, explicating her ideas through her biography and vice versa.

BIOGRAPHICAL TREATMENTS OF SIMONE WEIL:

Francine de Plessix Gray, *Simone Weil* (Viking Penguin, 2001).

Palle Yourgrau, *Simone Weil* (Reaktion Books, 2011).

NON-FICTION DISCUSSIONS OF COMPLEX SUFFERING AND INTERVENTION:

Garret Keizer, *Helping: The Original Human Dilemma* (HarperOne, 2005).

Tracy Kidder, *Rough Sleepers* (Random House, 2023).

William Styron, *Darkness Visible: A Memoir of Madness* (Random House, 1990).

MOVING FICTIONAL TREATMENTS OF AFFLICTION AND COMPLEX SUFFERING:

Lisa Genova, *Still Alice* (Gallery Books, 2009).

Graham Greene, *A Burnt-Out Case* (first published in 1969 by William Heinemann; reprint Penguin Books, 1992).

William Kennedy, *Ironweed: A Novel* (Penguin Books, 1984).

William Trevor, "Sitting with the Dead," *Selected Stories* (Viking Penguin, 2010).

Questions for Reflection and Group Discussion

1. Affliction is a complex form of suffering that uproots a life by damaging a person physically, psychologically, socially, and spiritually. Do you know people who have experienced affliction? If not, are there people less proximate to you that you surmise may be afflicted? How are their stories similar or different from Bill Miller's?

2. In Chapter 4, the author says that "Simone Weil tells us that the line between suffering and sorrow (however deep, violent, and lasting) and affliction is like the boiling point of water. The frog in the proverbial pot goes from comfortable to incapacitated without ever knowing it's cooked. Thus too, affliction sneaks up on its victims." At what point (or points) do you think that Bill Miller's suffering crosses from suffering to affliction?

3. In her epilogue, the author throws doubt on the legitimacy of question 2, saying, "The point of pondering affliction is not so that we can accurately sort humanity into two camps: the afflicted and those who are not. Instead, becoming sensitive to the possibility of affliction makes us treat each human being we encounter—especially those we find least prepossessing—as having a depth beyond our ken. As a mystery, not to be solved, but to be saluted." How would

you put her point in your own words? To what extent do you agree with her?

4. Which of Simone Weil's views that you encountered in this book did you find most insightful? Did you find any of them disturbing or objectionable?

5. Dialysis extends Bill Miller's life by six years but is also a significant source of his suffering and, possibly, of his affliction. Discuss how modern medicine, as practiced in Western and Westernized societies, can be a two-edged sword.

6. There are a few things in life that, even amid suffering, make Bill happy (some, for example, include helping a woman in his rehab facility, food, and caring for his cat Little Willy). What do you make of this?

7. Have you been in a situation where you've tried to help someone who was afflicted? In what ways was that more challenging than helping someone who was experiencing a less complex form of suffering?

8. In what ways does the existence of affliction affect your views about or relationship with God?

9. Do you think that Christians have special obligations to the afflicted? Why or why not? If so, what are they?

10. What social structures do you think make affliction more likely? What social structures help prevent or lessen affliction? How do race, class and gender, as enacted in your society, affect proneness to affliction?

11. Medical professionals talk about people who live with smokers being secondhand smokers. What might secondhand affliction involve?

12. Do you think that any of Bill and Carol's other family members (their father Wes, mother Vera, or sister Diana) experienced affliction, or did their sufferings never rise to that level? What factors are relevant to your answer?

13. Bill becomes increasingly withdrawn toward the end of his life. In what ways is such withdrawal a symptom of affliction? When is withdrawal itself a mute cry for help?

14. This is a tale of two siblings told from one sibling's point of view. How do you think Bill might have told this story differently? How do you think he viewed his sister Carol at crucial junctures in the story?

15. In her epilogue, the author says, "To clearly see the afflicted is not only to agonize with them, but to see that nothing protects you from becoming like them." Do you think that anyone, under certain circumstances, could become afflicted, or are some people immune? If the latter, what contributes to their immunity?

16. How did your experiences during the COVID pandemic affect your views about your own susceptibility to affliction? How does the increase in climate-related natural disasters and global political unrest affect your thinking about affliction?